TO
SHIFT
A NATION

HOW THE BODY OF CHRIST CAN EFFECTIVELY
PROMOTE CHANGE IN CANADA

— CRAIG DOCKSTEADER —

ISBN: 978-1-4866-2490-4
eBook ISBN: 978-1-4866-2491-1

Word Alive Press
119 De Baets Street Winnipeg, MB R2J 3R9
www.wordalivepress.ca

WORD ALIVE
—P R E S S—

Cataloguing in Publication information can be obtained from Library and Archives Canada.

To my wife, Gail, whose love, patience, encouragement, and unfaltering commitment made it possible to walk the roads that have led us to this place. Without your vision and sacrifice, this journey would have never been taken and these words would have never been written.

Hebrews 11:10

CONTENTS

ACKNOWLEDGEMENT

I OWE A debt of gratitude to my friend, former colleague, and mentor, Kevin P. Avram. As founder of the Canadian Taxpayers Federation and co-founder of the Centre for Prairie Agriculture, Kevin's leadership, sacrifice, and insights into how constructive change happens in society were deeply formative in the development of my own.

PREFACE

FOR MORE THAN thirty years, God has taken my wife and I on a journey that has profoundly impacted our understanding of the process of change and the role of the church in society. Even as Canada was sliding in the wrong direction, we witnessed first-hand as a few seemingly immovable policies began to shift in a better direction. We saw governments that had stubbornly refused to listen to the people change their minds and alter their course. We watched as people who felt helpless began to feel empowered. We saw oppressive darkness give way to hope, and hope give way to light. Within the limited sphere that we were engaged in during those years, we saw things change.

This experience marked us deeply. It transformed our understanding of how change happens in a nation and opened our eyes to see that our nation does not need to continue on its current path. There is hope!

From the things that we have seen, the things that we have learned, and what we read in scripture, we are convinced that God wants to once again shift our nation. But the key to that shift is his church—his ecclesia. We must begin to understand his strategy, his ways, his priorities, and we must choose to embrace them. If we do, it will amaze us what he can do.

This journey is not for the faint of heart. Some of your ideas might be challenged, and you might find yourself being dragged outside of your comfort zone. But it will be worth it. There is no obligation to agree with what you read here—only an invitation to come on a journey and let God speak to you.

I encourage you to be like the Bereans (Acts 17:11) and examine the scriptures to see if what is written here is true. Nobody has the whole picture, and nobody has it all figured out. What I share with you in these pages I offer with humility and with hope that it will not only challenge you but also encourage you to believe again for the future of our nation.

INTRODUCTION

IT'S DIFFICULT TO capture in words the anxiety and frustration many Canadian Christians are feeling these days. Over the last sixty years, Canada has gone from being a nation that was friendly toward Christian values to one where these same values are now either openly under attack or already trampled underfoot.

Prayer has been removed from schools, the rights of the unborn have been obliterated, marriage has been redefined, euthanasia has been legalized, marijuana is being normalized, society is hypersexualized, children are being taught that they can choose their gender, the rights of parents are being eroded, Christian organizations are being denied government funding because they won't endorse abortion, Christian universities are being restricted because of their convictions about sexuality and marriage—and this is just the beginning of the list. The simple fact is that Canada has changed. It is no longer the country of our grandparents.

In his work *Government Support for Religious Practice*, Professor Richard Moon wrote the following:

> A generation ago, it was not uncommon to hear Canada described as a Christian country. This was an acknowledgement that most Canadians adhered to some form of Christianity but also that the values

and practices of public life were shaped by the Christian faith. [But today] State support for the practices and values of a particular religion (or religion in general) is now viewed as a form of religious discrimination or an illegitimate imposition of religion.[1]

In other words, Canada has shifted. We can no longer consider ourselves a Christian nation. The truth is, we never were a Christian nation, but it may have seemed like we were because Christianity had state preference in Canada. Now we are just another minority voice. It's worth lingering on this thought for a moment to let it sink in, because this reality seems to be lost on many Christians: We are now just another minority voice. We no longer have the voice or the influence we once did.

This shift is the result of numerous factors, including the gradual dissociation of the functions of church and state in Canada, the move toward urbanization and industrialization, the growth of religious diversity, and the fact that Canada is no longer predominantly Christian. Whereas "at the time of Confederation in 1867, the concept of religious neutrality implied primarily respect for Christian denominations," [2] this is clearly no longer the case.

The Ontario Human Rights Commission puts it this way:

Scholars chart at least three main phases in Canada's historic response to governing religious diversity. These move along a continuum from a single (Catholic and then Anglican) state-supported church with a virtual religious monopoly on public culture and institutions toward a more inclusive current-day secular, multicultural approach.

These eras have been generally described as:
• 1608–1841: European Catholics and Protestants sought to transplant their forms of Christianity

to Canada through a state-supported Christian church, with little religious freedom.

- 1841–1960: Plural or shadow Christian establishment prevailed. While there was no official state church, there was a Christian culture and state cooperation with a limited number of "respectable" Christian churches (Anglican, Presbyterian, Methodist/United, Baptist and Roman Catholic churches).
- 1960–present: Society became more secular, with greater "separation of church and state," and an overtly multicultural approach to religion.[3]

Christians today find themselves in a nation they never envisioned, with a future that seems very uncertain. How we respond now is critical. Will we withdraw from the public square or will we re-engage? Will we be wise or will we be reckless? Will we be strategic or will we stumble? Will we be carnal or will we be spiritual? What we do now will determine the future we leave for our children and their children.

PART ONE

Pursuing National Change

> *"Now a new king arose over Egypt, who did not know
> Joseph ..."* (Exodus 1:8, AMP)

LIFE HAD BEEN good for Israel. They had just come through a time of blessing, favour, and prosperity in which they had enjoyed a privileged position in Egyptian society. God had used Joseph to first warn the pharaoh of the coming drought and then to provide the strategy and leadership necessary to ensure that Egypt not only survived but thrived in the midst of that drought.

For the next generation, Israel flourished in the favour that followed. Those in government were keenly aware of the value Joseph, and thus Israel, had brought to the nation, so they gave them the best land in the country on which to raise their families and flocks. But that was about to end. The memory of the past had dimmed, and Israel was now perceived as a threat to Egyptian society that needed to be controlled.

Somewhere, something had slipped. The memory of what had happened had faded. The thankfulness for the blessings that had come to Egypt because of Joseph had slowly dimmed until it was gone. Perhaps it would have been different if someone else from Israel had risen to carry on Joseph's ministry to the nation. But nobody did. Perhaps this was the will of God. Or perhaps they were just too happy to be in the prime land of Goshen and were busy raising their flocks and their families. Perhaps they were comfortable and enjoying the blessings that had come their way, oblivious to the fact that these were all quietly slipping away.

Regardless of why it happened, when you read the story from the first chapter of Exodus, you see that the transition was abrupt. The slide may have been slow, but the shift was sudden. There seems to have been little warning. Something had changed, and they didn't notice until it was too late. I would propose that the church in Canada today is in a similar position. Something has shifted, and we need to see it and understand how to respond before it's too late. Consider the parallels: Where once the church in Canada enjoyed a favoured position, this is gone. Where once there was an appreciation of what Christian values brought to society, this too appears to be almost gone.

Canada was never a "Christian" nation, but undeniably the first Christians to come here did so either to find a place where they could worship in freedom or because they were compelled to bring the gospel of Christ to others. They were intent on building a society where their faith could flourish and where they could freely share that faith with others. The church built schools and hospitals, cared for the poor, and gave generously to the needs around them in order to make society a better place for everyone.[4]

But somewhere along the way we grew comfortable. As the government moved in to take care of education, health care, and the poor, Christians grew more and more absorbed in other things. Mostly our own things. And while many Christians still carry a heart for the gospel and for society, as a whole we have clearly slipped. Our focus has become primarily about ourselves—our lives, our churches, our families, our careers, our financial security, our holidays, our welfare.

Without even knowing it, we are perilously close to an Exodus 1:8 situation: While everything seemed pretty good on the surface, something was shifting underneath. The very values that helped to form the foundation of a free and democratic country—Christian values—are starting to be perceived as a threat to the freedom of others. And unless something changes, our freedoms will begin to be limited in order to protect others from this threat—just like the nation of Israel experienced after Joseph died.

Some would say that this limiting of our freedoms has already begun. If so, then we have less time than we thought. This is not a time to shrug and carry on with business as usual. We are being awakened, and if we insist on going back to sleep because it's more comfortable, we can be certain that we will suddenly wake up in a place where we don't want to be.

This raises numerous questions: What should we do? How do we go about effectively promoting change in the nation? Are we able to speak freely? What is the role of prayer? Should we run for public office? Should we support a political party that promotes non-Christian policies? What exactly do we do and how does this work? These are some of the questions we will explore in the coming chapters.

CHAPTER ONE

Finding Our Way

WHEN MOST CHRISTIANS think of creating change in a nation, they think of political change. They think of electing a different government, prime minister, or member of Parliament. But it hasn't always been this way. At one time, the general attitude amongst the church was that Christians had no business getting involved in politics or any other role in the public square. As far as the world went, the church's only job was evangelism and discipleship. Get the lost saved and get them into the church.

Some people took this even further, convinced that attempting to change society was basically carnal (not to mention hopeless) and that the best thing we could do was get people saved and shelter them in the church, because everything was just going to get worse and worse. There seemed to be no vision to impact society. Our job was to hunker down, rescue as many people as possible, and wait for Jesus to come back.

Perhaps this was because Christians were largely unconcerned with how the nation was being governed at the time. Nobody was threatening to take away religious freedom, and the nation was still largely defined by Judeo-Christian values, so there was little need to get involved. Others were handling things and it seemed to be going just fine. As far as many Christians were concerned, ministry was found only in the church, and there was no concept of being called to serve in the public square.

But at some point, this attitude started to shift.

In the United States, William F. Buckley's famous statement—"I'd rather be governed by the first two thousand people in the Boston telephone directory than by the two thousand people on the faculty of Harvard University"—foreshadowed the changing sentiment. This view was not anti-intellectual but rather rooted in the conviction that the wisdom and views of the average person should be reflected in public policy and political decisions.

Over the next thirty years, from the early 1960s through the 1980s, the conventional thinking that politics should be left to the ruling class was consistently challenged through things such as the rise of the civil rights movement, the hippie counterculture, anti-war protests, student activism, and anti-establishment voices.

By the 1980s, British Prime Minister Margaret Thatcher and US President Ronald Reagan had been elected to office on populist-sounding platforms, which popularized this sentiment further. Their grassroots, folksy styles of leadership appealed to the common sense of the average person. At this time the US also saw the rise of Jerry Falwell's "Moral Majority." The movement encouraged Christians and everyday people who held "traditional values" to raise their voices on political issues and stand up and be counted. Falwell's efforts were controversial because they contradicted the popular American Christian understanding that there should be a separation between religion and politics, but it heralded an awakening amongst Christians to the responsibility of being informed and involved in the public square. The "religious right" had begun to flex their muscles.

As usual, however, Canada lagged behind. Perhaps it was our natural deference to authority or our propensity to apologize for merely having a differing opinion, but the same mobilization of the grassroots didn't begin to materialize in Canada until the late 1980s.

A multitude of factors contribute to societal shifts, but when we consider what began to awaken Christians in Canada to get involved in the public square, one undeniable catalyst was the rise of the Reform Party. The Reform Party was formed largely in response to western alienation, but over time it transformed into a movement that championed a grassroots, populist approach to political leadership and garnered national appeal.

People were tired of the elitism demonstrated by federal political parties of all stripes and the failure of politicians to reflect the values and common sense of the average person. The Reform Party began attracting political candidates who were not career politicians but instead run-of-the-mill people who wanted to influence constructive change and see a shift in the direction the country was going. This included a sharp increase in the number of Christians joining the political party and running for federal public office under its banner. It wasn't a coordinated or organized effort; it was an awakening amongst Christians that they had a societal responsibility to be engaged and active in the political decisions that affected society. There was an increasing awareness that God has called his people to impact society rather than separate themselves from it, and the grassroots approach of the Reform Party provided an opportunity and a vehicle to do just that.

But it was more than that. In Preston Manning, the church saw a Christian who was passionate in his vision for a better Canada and was using the public square to press for policies to realize that. Preston Manning was followed by Stockwell Day, and then by Stephen Harper, who were all unapologetic about their Christian faith. Many Christians began to see a place for themselves in the public square. As parts of the church in Canada began to take hold of this newfound vision—that their involvement in the public square could make a difference—a sense of momentum began to build, and optimism began to grow.

Between 2000 and 2015, the anticipation that Christians were on the right track and on the verge of seeing significant changes in the nation was palpable. Christian organizations were formed to help mobilize, equip, support, and release Christians into the public square. A focus on prayer for the nation and for government began to take root and flourish. Conferences, gatherings, and regular prayer meetings were held on and off Parliament Hill, which addressed the need to shift the direction of the nation. Efforts were made to find and support Christian candidates for public office and get them elected. Those who couldn't run themselves were encouraged to get involved with the campaigns of those who could by volunteering and supporting them financially. All of this was necessary and welcome. It was a refreshing and encouraging change from the sleepy days of yesteryear when Christians had all but abandoned the public square. But it wasn't enough.

I still recall the deep disappointment in 2015 when Stephen Harper was not re-elected as Prime Minister. Even though many Christians didn't view themselves as necessarily partisan, they found that the views and values of the Conservative Party most closely aligned with their own. Consequently, there was a significant push amongst believers to support the Conservative election campaign through both prayer and participation. When the Conservatives lost that election, many Christians who had worked so hard and believed so strongly were devastated and disillusioned.

Rather than getting better, things got worse. The new Liberal government began to slowly unwind many of the gains made under Stephen Harper's leadership and introduced policies that would shift the nation in a direction most Christians found troubling. From the legalization of marijuana, to assisted suicide, to the erasure of any connection between anatomical sex and perceived gender, to the renewed funding for abortion in foreign countries, to the closure of the Office of Religious Freedom—the changes were alarming.

After recovering from their initial disillusionment and disappointment, the response of many Christians was to double-down and level-up. They doubled down with even greater determination that all we needed was more of what we'd been doing before: more prayer, more activism, more involvement, more sacrifice. They levelled-up by torquing the rhetoric even tighter: Unless the Liberal party was defeated, the country would be ruined and never achieve its destiny in God. In the same way that Dietrich Bonhoeffer stood up to Nazi Germany, Christians were supposed to resist and defeat the Liberal government through prayer, proclamations, and political activity.

There was growing determination and confidence that the 2019 federal election needed to be, and would be, a turning point. But it never happened. Instead, Canada elected a minority Liberal government supported by a trio of political parties that were even further to the left. Hardly a recipe for reformation. When the election outcome in 2021 was basically a carbon copy of the 2019 election results, the mood darkened further. Despite all of the prayer, effort, and time invested, things fell short. Again and again and again.

CHAPTER TWO

What Went Wrong?

SO WHAT WENT wrong? To use a sports analogy, at least we've been on the field. But the bad news is that we're losing every game along with the entire season. Why?

After each election, every political party takes some time to look at the results and conduct a post-mortem: What went right? What went wrong? What needs to change? Different views and theories emerge, and it's a good exercise because, at a minimum, it pinpoints the most obvious mistakes and ensures that they're not repeated. Sometimes it just uncovers minor tweaks that need to be made, and other times the process reveals needed systemic changes.

If we conducted such a reflection of the church's involvement in the public square over the last thirty years and were to ask, "Despite all the increased awareness, prayer and participation, why do we appear to be losing ground rather than gaining it?", we'd get many different answers. But I propose that two critical factors have contributed to our lack of success.

1. Looking for a King

Participation in politics and the public square is an imperative for Christians. But in their quest to make a difference, many well-intentioned Christians have fallen into the age-old trap of looking for a king—where we begin to think and act like societal change is imposed from the top down.

This isn't new. The people of God have been falling into this trap since Old Testament times. In 1 Samuel 8, the Israelites demand that the prophet Samuel give them a king to rule over them. They've decided that having a king will better protect their freedoms and ensure that justice is upheld in the nation.

On the surface, they had a legitimate point to make. Samuel was getting old, and his sons were in line to take over his role as judge. But his sons had a well-known track record of being corrupt, which concerned the people greatly.

> When Samuel grew old, he appointed his sons as Israel's leaders. The name of his firstborn was Joel and the name of his second was Abijah, and they served at Beersheba. But his sons did not follow his ways. They turned aside after dishonest gain and accepted bribes and perverted justice. (1 Samuel 8:1–3, NIV)

There were serious shortcomings in the leadership of Israel. Not only were Samuel's sons clearly lacking integrity, but even more alarming was the fact that Samuel was still willing to appoint them as his successors. The nation looked at this and found it unacceptable. They saw how other nations were governed and decided that they'd be better off adopting the same model. They needed a king.

> Then all the elders of Israel gathered together and came to Samuel at Ramah and said to him, "Behold, you are old and your sons do not walk in your ways. Now appoint for us a king to judge us like all the nations." (1 Samuel 8:4–5, ESV)

Although understandable, the nation's request for a king was an outright repudiation of God's rulership over them. Rather than placing their confidence in Him, they looked elsewhere for their security. And as scripture shows, this didn't go over well:

> But the thing displeased Samuel when they said, "Give us a king to judge us." And Samuel prayed to the Lord. And the Lord said to Samuel, "Obey the voice of the people in all that they say to you, for they have not rejected you, but they have rejected me from being king over them." (1 Samuel 8:6–7, ESV)

Samuel proceeded to warn them that appointing a king would mean less freedom, not more.

> [Samuel] said, "This is what the king who will reign over you will claim as his rights: He will take your sons and make them serve with his chariots and horses, and they will run in front of his chariots. Some he will assign to be commanders of thousands and commanders of fifties, and others to plough his ground and reap his harvest, and still others to make weapons of war and equipment for his chariots. He will take your daughters to be perfumers and cooks and bakers. He will take the best of your fields and vineyards and olive groves and give them to his attendants. He will take a tenth of your grain and of your vintage and give it to his officials and attendants. Your male and female servants and the best of your cattle and donkeys he will take for his own use. He will take a tenth of your flocks, and you yourselves will become his slaves. When that day comes, you will cry out for relief from the king you have chosen, but the Lord will not answer you in that day." (1 Samuel 8:11–18, NIV)

The consequences of their choice were stark, but the Israelites were insistent. Their desire for a sense of security and stability trumped Samuel's warning, and they insisted on having a king regardless.

> But the people refused to listen to Samuel. "No!" they said. "We want a king over us. Then we will be like all the other nations, with a king to lead us and to go out before us and fight our battles." (1 Samuel 8:19–20, NIV)

The people of Israel's mistake wasn't their desire for godly leadership. It was their rejection of God's pattern for godly leadership and their determination to replace it with a different model. In doing so, Israel made two critical errors that would haunt them for centuries. First, they shifted their expectations for the preservation of their freedom and security from God to their political leadership. Second, they began to shift the responsibility for righteousness within the nation from themselves to their leaders. In other words, it became all about the leader. Their paradigm had shifted. Whereas God had placed the responsibility for the preservation of a godly society on the people, they were now convinced that this was an ineffective model, and they pursued a top-down vision of reform.

I would argue that this is precisely what has happened within the church of Canada. As much as our theology might say something different, our actions, attitudes, and speech testify against us, revealing that we believe the government is responsible for the state of the nation, not the people. This isn't to suggest that good government isn't important. It is. But in Canada, like most Western democracies, government is a reflection of the state of the nation, not the rudder that determines the direction of the nation. If we don't recognize this truth, we'll make the same mistake as the Israelites: We'll believe that the problems of the nation can be resolved by changing the leadership. It's like demanding different fruit without addressing the root. And it simply doesn't work.

God warned the Israelites of this. They thought that having a king would fix their problems and that the responsibility for the welfare of the nation would now rest with the king rather than with them. But God made it clear that by choosing a king, they had not only rejected him, but they would also still be responsible for the state of the nation. It was the people and whether or not they followed God with all their hearts who would determine the health of the nation, not the leader.

> And now behold the king whom you have chosen, for whom you have asked; behold, the Lord has set a king over you. If you will fear the Lord and serve him and obey his voice and not rebel against the commandment of the Lord, and if both you and the king who reigns over you will follow the Lord your God, it will be well. But if you will not obey the voice of the Lord, but rebel against the commandment of the Lord, then the hand of the Lord will be against you and your king. (1 Samuel 12:13–15, ESV)

Samuel makes it clear that the responsibility for the welfare of the nation rests in the hands of the people. If they choose to rebel against God, then the hand of the Lord will be against both them and their king.

We see this borne out under the reign of Israel's first king, Saul. Israel was in the midst of a standoff with the Philistines, in which they were seriously outnumbered: "*The Philistines assembled to fight Israel, with three thousand chariots, six thousand charioteers, and soldiers as numerous as the sand on the seashore*" (1 Samuel 13:5a, NIV). The Israelites were terrified and began to flee and hide.

> When the Israelites saw that their situation was critical and that their army was hard pressed, they hid in

> caves and thickets, among the rocks, and in pits and cisterns. Some Hebrews even crossed the Jordan to the land of Gad and Gilead." (1 Samuel 13:6–7, NIV)

The people had their eyes on man, rather than on God, and so were full of fear rather than faith. When Saul saw this, he was shaken. To try and rectify the situation, he took matters into his own hands. Rather than pointing them back to God, he permitted them to look to him as their source and tried to fix it.

> [Saul] waited seven days, the time appointed by Samuel. But Samuel did not come to Gilgal, and the people were scattering from him. So Saul said, "Bring the burnt offering here to me, and the peace offerings." And he offered the burnt offering. As soon as he had finished offering the burnt offering, behold, Samuel came. And Saul went out to meet him and greet him. Samuel said, "What have you done?" And Saul said, "When I saw that the people were scattering from me, and that you did not come within the days appointed, and that the Philistines had mustered at Michmash, I said, 'Now the Philistines will come down against me at Gilgal, and I have not sought the favor of the Lord.' So I forced myself, and offered the burnt offering." (1 Samuel 13:8–12, ESV)

It was a critical mistake for Saul, one that would make him ineligible to continue as king of Israel. Although he was king, he was not permitted to offer sacrifices—this was a priestly duty, reserved exclusively for the Levitical priesthood. Saul knew this, which was why he was initially waiting for Samuel to show up and offer the sacrifice. But as the people began to waver in their faith, Saul buckled and stepped over the line he was never to cross. The root of

Saul's failure was a direct consequence of the people's lack of faith in God. His failure grew out of the people's failure, not the other way around.

We see this again in 1 Samuel 15. In this situation, Israel had been instructed to attack the Amalekites and completely destroy them and all their possessions. But in the midst of their victory, the Israelites decided they wanted to keep some of the spoils for themselves. Saul relented and allowed them to do it. When Samuel arrived on the scene, he confronted Saul, and Saul confessed: "... *I have sinned, for I have transgressed the commandment of the Lord and your words, because I feared the people and obeyed their voice*" (1 Samuel 15:24, ESV).

Notice that this failure was once again precipitated by the failure of the people to believe and obey God. Saul was held responsible for his part, but the entire nation would pay the price as they endured dissension, strife, and civil war for many years to come.

This is a pattern that the people of God continue to repeat to this day. Failing to realize that the welfare of the nation turns on the will of the people, not its leaders, we shift our expectations for the preservation of our freedom and security from God to the government. We mistakenly believe that by changing the government, we can change the trajectory of the nation. While it's imperative that we strive for good government, we must never lose sight of the fact that government is a mirror of the state of the nation, not a lever that determines it. Failing to realize this guarantees our ineffectiveness in the public square.

2. Ignoring the Undercurrents

The second critical factor that has contributed to the church's ineffectiveness in shifting the nation over the last thirty years is that while our attention was locked on what the government was doing, we ignored the fact that society was moving swiftly in the wrong direction.

When things look like they're going your way, it's easy to miss the undercurrents. This happens to political parties all the time. When they're in power, they enjoy the fact that their message is usually the loudest. Because they are the government, they hold the biggest megaphone, and a sense of overconfidence can easily set in. It's not that they're unaware of contrary positions to theirs, but the politicization of the public debate creates a polarized conversation, where neither side is hearing the other. A degree of arrogance usually sets in, and people with contrary views are dismissed rather than listened to.

But the average person does listen. They're not fundamentally partisan, and when legitimate concerns or questions are raised about the direction of a government or how they're conducting themselves, people pay attention. While the party in government and its supporters may tend to shrug it off, those less entrenched in partisanship don't. They begin to shift in their loyalties and voting intentions— sometimes without even saying anything.

A colleague told me the story of a former Saskatchewan MLA who was first elected in 1982. That year the Saskatchewan Conservative party swept to power in the province, taking fifty-seven of the province's sixty-four seats. It was the first time that the Conservatives had won provincially since 1929. At the next provincial election, in 1986, that MLA won his seat again, and the Conservatives held on to their majority but were reduced to thirty-six seats. But by 1991, things had changed. The MLA remained quite confident because he was well liked in his constituency and had won both the 1982 and the 1986 elections easily. No one who had supported him in the previous elections told him they weren't going to vote for him this time around, and he was certain that his personal credibility and good reputation would assure him a third term.

But partway through the election campaign, he noticed that people were avoiding him. He told my colleague that one day as he was walking down the sidewalk of a small town in his riding, some of his supporters were heading toward him on the sidewalk but then crossed over to the other side in an obvious attempt to avoid meeting him. At that point he realized something had shifted.

The truth is, it had been shifting for months, if not years. Under the Conservative government, the provincial debt had ballooned, and the standard of living had dropped. The people were no longer confident that the Conservatives could properly govern the province and manage its economy. Yet they never saw it coming until it was too late. This MLA ended up losing badly, and his party was almost obliterated, being reduced to only ten seats. Stories like this aren't uncommon, and they usually happen because we're looking at the wrong things and miss the signs that something is shifting.

This has been the story of the church over the last thirty years. If we had been in touch with the state of society around us, we wouldn't be surprised by the changes taking place in our nation's moral fabric and legislative framework. We wouldn't be shocked to see the government going to great lengths to erase the connection between biological sex and gender. We wouldn't be shocked to see them expanding access to assisted suicide. We wouldn't be surprised that after legalizing marijuana, they quickly began discussing the possibility of legalizing other street drugs. We wouldn't be surprised that the momentum of the legislative agenda has been going in the wrong direction.

But we were surprised because we were spending too much time looking at the wrong things. Failing to see the real roots of what was happening in our society, we lay the blame squarely at the feet of the government and focus the bulk of our attention there. This has been a costly mistake.

For over thirty years, my full-time work has been in the field of advocacy and public policy. For much of that time, I've seen the church more passionate about winning an election than winning the lost. I've seen more partisanship than discipleship, and more prayer for government than care for the broken. The declining state of the nation has consistently been attributed to the performance of the Prime Minister rather than the effectiveness of the church.

Don't get me wrong, Christians should be fully engaged in the public square. But if we're obsessing about politics and policy when we're not passionate for Jesus and consumed with his heart for the lost, discipling the nation, and seeing heaven come to earth, we are deceiving ourselves. It's like weeding a garden we forgot to plant something in: No matter how hard we work, there still won't be a harvest.

At the end of the day, both of these factors—looking for a king and ignoring the undercurrents—have contributed to the church's failure to shift the direction of the nation. The direction we were going thirty years ago is still the direction we're headed today. The only difference is that rather than getting better, things have gotten worse. If we're going to change that trajectory, we need to acknowledge this fact. And then we need to go back to the drawing board to understand how change happens in a nation and what role the church plays in making that happen.

CHAPTER THREE

When Change Happens

WHEN MY WIFE and I began our journey of promoting change in the public square, our primary challenge was not convincing politicians. It was convincing people that change was even possible. For the most part, people had lost hope. They no longer believed that they had any power to influence change. When we'd encourage people to speak up and make their voices heard, they'd respond with, "What good will it do? I'm only one voice." They felt helpless, powerless, and alone. We had to first restore their hope that something could be done and that their involvement was critical.

Naturally, not everyone was convinced, but some were. And over time, the momentum and the movement toward change grew. Little victories led to larger victories, and larger victories led to greater influence. Hope was rekindled, and change began to take place where it had previously seemed impossible. It was a journey that would impact us deeply.

SASKATCHEWAN: FROM DEFICIT TO BALANCE

In the late 1980s and early 90s, Saskatchewan was plummeting into debt. After inheriting the leadership of a province that had balanced its budget for thirty-five of the previous thirty-eight years, Premier Grant Devine brought that record to a screeching halt and launched the province into twelve consecutive years of spending deficits.

In fairness, during Devine's time as Premier, the province experienced the worst droughts since the "Dirty Thirties," faced crippling mortgage rates of up to 19 per cent, and saw the price of oil and agricultural commodities collapse. The government's response was to ratchet up spending through things such as subsidized mortgages, matching grants for home renovations, and increased support for agriculture programs.

The result was a staggering debt load that grew annually and began to seriously impact Saskatchewan's credit rating. From 1986 to 1992, the province was downgraded five times by Standard & Poors credit rating agency, and three times by Moody's Investors Service. When the credit rating dropped to BBB+, the City of Regina's employee pension fund could no longer buy Saskatchewan government bonds because they weren't considered to be "investment grade."

While most people in the province were supportive of the government's spending spree, some were not. In 1989, a small organization was formed called the Association of Saskatchewan Taxpayers (AST). Tasked with the job of "promoting the responsible and efficient use of tax dollars," the AST set out to shift the fiscal policy of the province from deficit financing back to balanced budgets.

When I started working for the AST in early 1991, the organization was barely a year old, yet it was already making waves in the province. Within two years, it had helped shift attitudes about government debt so much that the socialist New Democratic Party won the provincial election on a platform of responsible financial management, promising to cut spending and balance the budget. It took four more years, but in fiscal year 1994/95, Saskatchewan posted its first surplus in twelve years and introduced balanced budget legislation.

It wouldn't be accurate to say that the AST was solely responsible for this shift in public policy, but there's no question that the organization played a significant role. This impact is documented, in part, in Troy Lanigan's book, *Fighting for Taxpayers.*[5] It tells the story of how the organization's success in Saskatchewan led to the formation of taxpayer associations in Alberta, British Columbia, Manitoba, and eventually across the country, becoming known as the Canadian Taxpayers Federation.

This was our first taste of being part of a significant shift in the nation. But it wouldn't be our last.

CANADIAN WHEAT BOARD: FROM MONOPOLY TO VOLUNTARY

Following the Taxpayers Association, I went on to co-found an organization called the Centre for Prairie Agriculture, which became known as the Prairie Centre. It had one goal: to see the Canadian Wheat Board's (CWB) monopoly powers removed so that farmer participation in the CWB could be voluntary.

The CWB had been created in 1935 and was given monopoly powers by the federal government in 1943 to keep the price of wheat from rising during World War II. After the war ended, the government retained the CWB's monopoly because the majority of farmers were leery of returning to a competitive system, and retaining the monopoly helped the government to fulfil its promise to provide cheap wheat to Britain as part of the post-war effort to rebuild.

As a government agency with monopoly powers, the CWB was the sole buyer and seller of prairie wheat and barley destined for human consumption from 1943 onward. Prairie farmers were forced by law to deliver their wheat or barley to the CWB, who would then sell it for them. The revenue from the sales (which was kept secret) was then averaged over the course of the year, and farmers were eventually paid in full for their grain deliveries—usually about eighteen months after delivering their produce to the CWB.

The problems with this system were enormous and economically significant, yet in 1994 when the Prairie Centre was just getting off the ground, the majority of farmers continued to support the monopoly. Polling results varied, but it would be accurate to say that the CWB enjoyed the support of approximately two-thirds of prairie farmers. The other third wanted the monopoly removed so that they would have the same marketing freedom for wheat and barley they already had for every other commodity they grew.

For the next nine years, the Prairie Centre worked to change this government policy. Although not the only organization working to do so, the Prairie Centre's impact promoting change on this issue was significant. By 2002, support for the CWB's monopoly status had significantly declined, with approximately one-third of farmers supporting the monopoly, and two-thirds of farmers wanting what had become known as "dual-marketing," in which farmers could choose for themselves where they sold their wheat and barley. Support for the monopoly had shifted, and the numbers were now reversed.

This shift in public support paved the way for the federal government to remove the CWB's monopoly in 2012. What had seemed impossible only a short time before had become a reality. A significant shift had once again taken place.

CREATING CHANGE: A STRATEGIC APPROACH

In both situations described above, change was far from guaranteed. The status quo was firmly entrenched, and the odds were not in our favour.

During the early days of the Prairie Centre, we would often receive hate mail, with our business reply envelopes (meant to be used by those who wanted to support the organization) returned to us filled with nasty letters, shredded paper, dirt, or worse. One of our field reps who canvassed rural areas and signed up supporters had a full can of paint thrown at his car as he was leaving the yard. He returned to the office with a smashed rear window, quite shaken up. Threats of physical violence were common but fortunately rarely acted upon.

We used to note how people's positions, especially on the Canadian Wheat Board's monopoly, were often more akin to a religious conviction than a fact-based conclusion. Such convictions were commonly handed down from generation to generation, and the stories that had been told by a father or grandfather were all the proof needed to cement a longstanding loyalty. Such deep-founded beliefs didn't move quickly or easily. Yet slowly, over time, attitudes began to soften and support for change began to grow. You could feel a shift taking place.

The biggest changes were always observable in communities that carried our weekly columns. Every week, we wrote a five-hundred-to-six-hundred-word commentary, which was distributed across the prairie provinces and published in about 20 per cent of weekly prairie newspapers. These columns would take one staff person two to three days to research and write, which for a small organization was a significant investment of resources. But they were a critical tool in creating awareness, providing information, and promoting discussion about the issues where change was needed.

When a field representative from the organization went into a community where our commentaries were being published on a regular basis, the difference in the reception was tangible. After returning to the same communities year after year, field reps would note how even those who were at first adamantly opposed to change were becoming more receptive. The ground was softening.

Over the nine years of its operation, the Prairie Centre distributed more than a million copies of its publications across the prairies. This was over and above the weekly commentaries. In every case, the objective was never to simply overpower someone with witty answers but to provide clear, accurate information on the issues in order to help people to come to an informed, defensible, and credible position. This is important. There is a common misunderstanding that change can and should happen quickly, but change always takes longer than you think it will and costs more than you expect it will. And the outcome is never as perfect as you envisioned. Creating change requires a strategic, disciplined focus. And understanding the process of change is critical to success.

CHAPTER FOUR

How Change Happens

WHEN YOU LOOK around the world or even here in Canada and see all the change taking place, it can be overwhelming. In an attempt to make sense of it all, people will adopt different theories of change. For example, some Christians take the view that everything is playing out exactly as God has foreordained it to happen, and we should just rejoice in his sovereignty, assured of Christ's imminent return. Others believe that the devil has somehow gained the upper hand and nothing can be done because we're in the end times. What is happening is exactly what the book of Revelation says will happen. Others exhort us that the problem lies in the fact that we're not praying enough or engaging in spiritual warfare. Still others blame it on the media, the education system, the government, the World Economic Forum, or the Antichrist himself. How does one make sense of all that is happening and the bewildering array of possible causes with only one lifetime to figure it all out? To be honest, it's not easy. But it begins with understanding the process of change.

UNDERSTANDING THE PROCESS OF CHANGE

Untold numbers of books have been written on the process of change. It's a complex, nuanced topic fraught with debate. Nonetheless, we need to tackle it. We're not going to delve deeply into the subject, but we do need to lay a basic framework to assist us in developing a strategy for how the body of Christ can effectively promote change in the nation.

The following model is but one framework in a sea of ideas. If you Google some of the phrases, you'll find endless variations as people apply similar principles to different sectors (e.g., organizational change, innovation, leadership, markets, economics, business, etc.). Arguments can be made to use a different matrix, but for our purposes, the following one serves well. Understanding it will help you make sense of the shifts that have happened, and need to happen, in our society.

Four Types of Change

In this matrix, there are four different types of change: directed change, organic change, radical change, and incremental change.

Directed change. Directed change happens because someone with the power to make change happen, uses it. This kind of change is top-down, centrally controlled, and imposed on others. It's power-centric because it derives its source from someone having the ability to make the change. This kind of change happens when the government passes a law or when someone is arrested by the police.

Organic change. Organic change happens because of a shift in what people believe. As beliefs change, society changes—this is organic change. It's voluntary, not imposed (like directed change), because people willingly choose to make or allow the change. It's value-centric, not power-centric, because it's driven by shifts in people's values and beliefs, not by someone's ability to impose change on others.

Radical change. Radical change is quick or large-scale. It happens suddenly or is very significant. It's episodic, meaning it occurs occasionally and at irregular and often unpredictable intervals.

Incremental change. Incremental change is what the name suggests—incremental and gradual. It happens in a series of steps or over a period of time. It's often difficult to determine when the change started or when it stopped. Unlike directed change, it can be difficult to attribute incremental change to a specific source or cause.

BUILDING THE FRAMEWORK

If we put these four types of change together on a chart, we can see how they relate to each other. For example, directed change is the opposite of organic change. So if we plot these on a horizontal line, directed change goes on one end, and organic change goes on the other (Illustration 1).

All change can be plotted on this line and is either directed or organic, or somewhere in between. Change can be partly organic and mostly directed, or it can be mostly organic and only partly directed. The result looks like this:

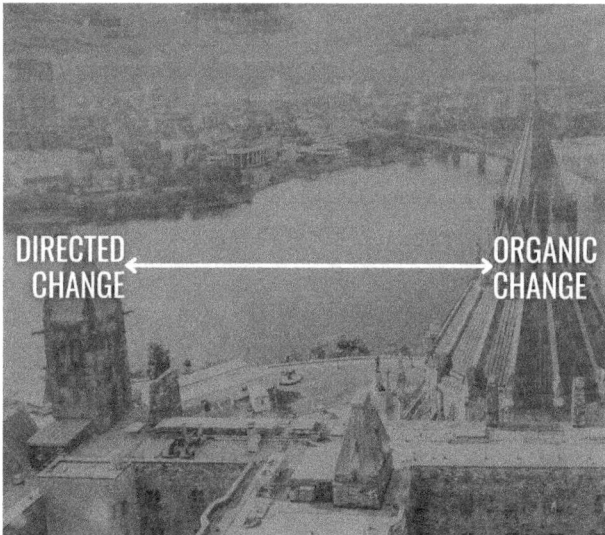

Illustration 1: Directed or organic change (source)

Similarly, radical change is the opposite of incremental change. Radical change happens quickly, and incremental change happens slowly. If we plot them on a vertical line with radical on the top and incremental on the bottom, it looks like the illustration below. Every instance of change can be plotted somewhere in between these two points.

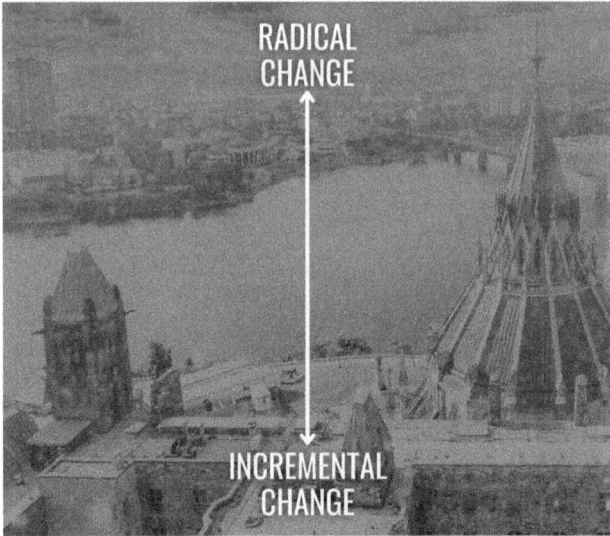

Illustration 2: Radical or incremental change (speed)

If we lay these two lines over top of each other, we end up with a grid that has four quadrants and looks like this:

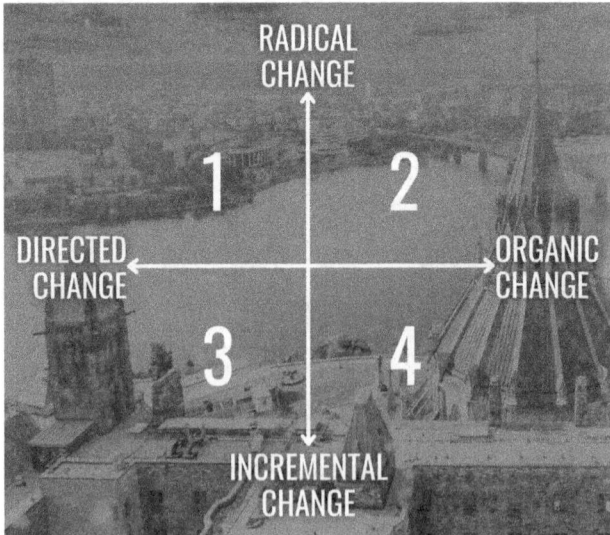

Illustration 3: The four quadrants of change

This is where things start to come together. The top left quadrant is radical and directed change, the top right is radical and organic change, the bottom left is directed and incremental change, and the bottom right is organic and incremental change. All change happens within one of these four quadrants.

Let's take a closer look.

Quadrant One: Radical and Directed Change

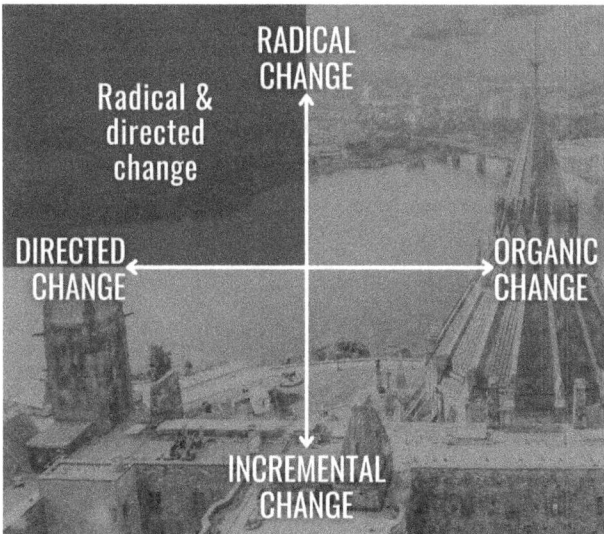

Radical and directed change happens quickly because someone has the power to impose the change. The most obvious example of this is change made by government, such as what happened during the COVID-19 pandemic. Due to what was feared to be a public health emergency, governments across the nation made sweeping, radical changes: businesses and schools were shut down, churches were closed, streets were empty, and malls were vacant.

The debate over whether these were the right decisions or taken in the right measure will probably never end. But it's a perfect illustration of radical and directed change: it happened quickly because someone had the power to impose the change.

Whenever an organization or special interest group says they want to see change, they're usually talking about radical and directed change. What they mean is that they want the government or the courts to force the change, and they almost always want it immediately. They hold demonstrations or launch legal challenges structured to compel those who hold the power of change to use it, while issuing angry press releases filled with strong statements condemning inaction.

Both during and after the pandemic, we saw an increase in organizations calling for the government to use this same power in other ways. Having seen how quickly change can happen in this quadrant, special interest groups rallied to demand that other societal issues be immediately resolved the same way. Action was demanded on social, environmental, and economic issues such as climate change, income disparity, education, labour, and more.

The World Economic Forum captured the essence of these demands, asserting that:

> ... the world must act jointly and swiftly to revamp all aspects of our societies and economies, from education to social contracts and working conditions. Every country, from the United States to China, must participate, and every industry, from oil and gas to tech, must be transformed. [6]

For those who support this agenda, the realization that a window of opportunity had opened to press for radical and directed change was intoxicating. But for those who saw danger in both the agenda and the process, the assertions were alarming.

In the following pages, we'll learn that radical and directed change, although attractive to those who want change, is fraught with danger and is unsustainable unless first supported at the grassroots level. When change is decoupled from organic and incremental change (quadrant four) it results in a disconnect between those in power and the average, everyday person. This disconnect becomes a fertile breeding ground for civil unrest, conspiracy theories, and a breakdown of trust in societal institutions. We are living this reality today.

Perhaps without realizing it, too much of the church has landed in this quadrant. Although we aren't necessarily issuing angry press releases, when it comes to praying for our nation, church prayer meetings often focus here. We ask God to change the law, change the policy, change the government, stop the Prime Minister, stop the opposition, prevent the law from passing, and so on. We're looking for radical and directed change—change from the top down and quick! We act like the key to changing the nation is changing the government.

Christians who focus on radical and directed change usually sound something like this:

- "Christians have the power to make the change; we just need to get involved."
- "We just need more Christian MPs/more pro-life MPs/more socially conservative MPs/et cetera in Parliament and then we can create change."
- "As Christians, we have the numbers. We simply need to mobilize the church."
- "The church in Canada is a sleeping giant. We need to awaken and activate Christians politically."

There is truth in each one of these statements. But without understanding how change happens, there's also room for significant error. The truth is, Christians should be awake and active and mobilized and involved in the political processes of our nation. In fact, without it, we can forget about seeing constructive change. But the error is thinking that this is the catalyst for shifting the nation. It is not.

Believing that the nation can be shifted by getting more Christians into public office is naive and dangerous. Such thinking alludes to the idea of creating a Christian "caliphate" and evidences a belief that Christians should aspire to use the power of the state to force people to adopt Christian values, habits, and activities. This is both offensive to the heart of the gospel and radically opposed to the biblical strategy for change (more on this in Part Two: God's Strategy for Change).

To top it off, it's a losing strategy. Every Christian Member of Parliament who shows up in Ottawa after winning an election quickly learns that they cannot change anything substantive without first having broad-based support at the grassroots level. And if they ignore this fact, they become what's known as a "one-term wonder." They simply don't survive the next election cycle. Christians need to be in public office, but we must not fall into the trap of thinking that this is the key to transforming the nation.

Quadrant Two: Radical and Organic Change

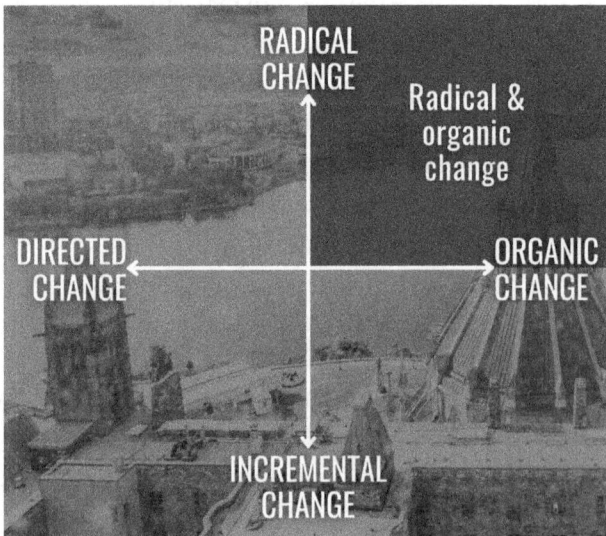

Radical and organic change happens quickly but takes place because of changing values or beliefs. Politically, it's unusual to have radical and organic change happen together because it means the change is both quick and driven from the bottom up. But it does happen. And when it does, it's usually messy and volatile, with uncertain outcomes.

An example of radical and organic change is what became known as the "Arab Spring." The Arab Spring began with demonstrations in Tunisia following the public self-immolation of Mohamed Bouazizi, a twenty-six-year-old Tunisian street vendor, in December of 2010. Mohamed had set himself on fire to protest the treatment he was receiving from government officials and subsequently died from his injuries. The resulting civil unrest led to the ousting of the Tunisian president only one month later, in January 2011. A wave of similar uprisings followed across North Africa and the Middle East, with other regimes toppling as well. This was radical and organic change. It happened very quickly and came from the bottom up.

The challenge with this type of change is that it usually brings unforeseeable consequences. In the Arab Spring, although citizens were protesting oppressive dictatorships and their lack of democratic freedoms, only the uprising in Tunisia resulted in a transition to a democratic government. Many of the other countries were either gripped by civil war or saw the vacuum of leadership give rise to extremist groups like ISIS.

The election of Donald Trump as President of the United States of America is another example of radical and organic change. This development was undeniably driven by masses of Americans who were anxious about the future and had lost confidence in the existing political establishment. Being outside of the political establishment, Donald Trump was able to step into this vacuum, win the confidence of the American people, and win the presidency. It was radical and organic; it happened quickly and came from the bottom up.

I have no interest in engaging in the polarized debate about whether Americans made the right or wrong choice in electing Donald Trump as President. But the aftermath in the following four years of his presidency demonstrates the volatility of radical and organic change. The division amongst the American people themselves fomented all kinds of unrest and gave opportunity to those with radical or questionable agendas. When radical and organic change happens, it can bring some undesirable results. It is highly unstable and not a strategy to be pursued by those who seek to constructively shift a nation.

Ironically, the church often finds itself in a place where it embraces this kind of change. To be clear, I am not referring to whether or not the church supported Donald Trump. I'm referring to the church's fixation with revival as the solution to the nation's problems. When the church advocates that all we need to fix the ills of society is for God to send a powerful revival, we are focusing on this quadrant. We view ourselves as largely unable to change anything unless God sovereignly intervenes and disrupts the nation's "business as usual" through a sweeping move of the Holy Spirit.

This isn't entirely wrong. In fact, revival is necessary and something we should all be longing and praying for. But to embrace it in isolation, on its own, as the key to societal reformation results in a church that is largely fatalistic rather than intentional. We end up spending all of our time trying to convince God to do something rather than doing what he has already given us to do. Furthermore, as can be seen from history, the results are largely temporary and the impact on society short-lived. Lasting, systemic change requires a different approach.

Quadrant Three: Directed and Incremental Change

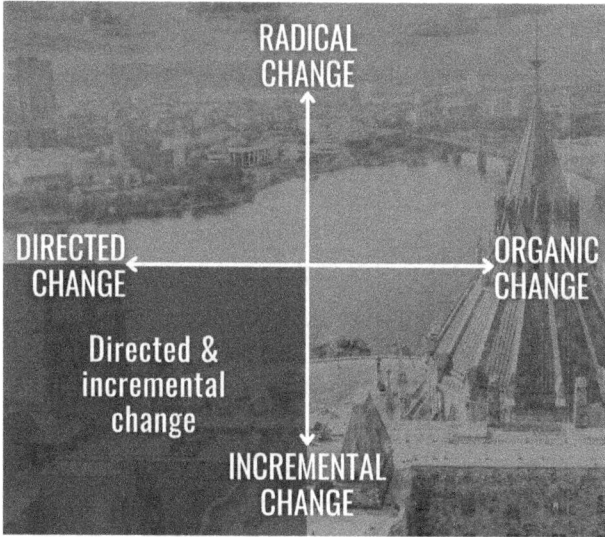

Next we have directed and incremental change. This is change made by those who hold the power to do so, but the change happens slowly over a period of time.

A good example of directed and incremental change is that which comes from lobbying the government. Lobbyists want the government to change something, so they work at convincing the government of the legitimacy of their position and the need for change. This process can take years or even decades as successive governments slowly become attuned to the need and sympathetic to the request. It usually happens over time and in small increments, and the source of the change comes from those who hold the power to make it.

But without organic change, directed change of a systemic kind is usually unsustainable. This is why most of the change in this quadrant focuses on micro policies—things that affect a small constituency of people within a specific, common sphere. It might be a tweaking of obscure regulations that only affect a specific industry, an amendment to existing legislation that improves it and better achieves its intent, or an altering of a zoning requirement on a municipal level that has little impact on most of the local population but a significant impact on a few. The list could go on, but you get the idea. Directed and incremental change is made by those who hold the power to do so, but it happens slowly over a period of time.

Quadrant 4: Organic and Incremental Change

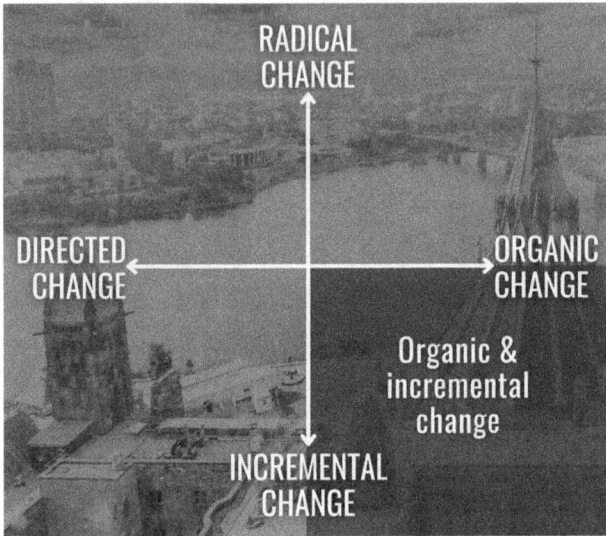

The fourth quadrant is organic and incremental change. This is where change happens slowly over time and is propelled by a shift in values or beliefs. In this case, change doesn't happen because someone forces it to take place but because people *want* change. And the reason they want change is because they see things differently than they used to.

When people's beliefs change, society changes. All we have to do is look at the last sixty years of societal changes in Canada to realize that this is the case. The steady deterioration of community standards and societal norms in our country has taken place primarily because people's beliefs have changed, not because government imposed these changes on the people. This is critical to understand. It's true that government can have a powerful impact on a nation and make changes that steer a country in the wrong direction. But in a democratic country, that only happens if the government has the permission of the people. And that permission is only granted when the majority of society thinks that the government is doing the right thing. In other words, the change must be in agreement with what the people believe.

This illustrates why organic and incremental change is the most effective, powerful, and permanent form of change: The focus is not on the symptoms, but on the roots. The focus is not on directly changing the policies or priorities of the government but on changing the beliefs and values of the people. Changing the beliefs of people will result in organic change, which politicians won't be able to refuse. It creates an unstoppable rising tide that cannot be turned.

The changes we saw take place in Saskatchewan and with the Canadian Wheat Board bore this out. It was not an overnight shift nor without significant cost on the part of those who were advocating for change. But over time, change began to happen, and for the same reason: The views of people had changed, and they began to actively press for change at the political and public policy levels, which reflected their new beliefs.

The climate change debate is a good illustration of this. Regardless of your position on the issue, the momentum for change is growing because a growing number of people are convinced that the climate is changing due to "anthropogenic greenhouse gases"—manmade carbon emissions.

Conspiracy theories abound, but the simple fact is that no one has the power to effect change on a global level unless they can first convince the majority of people that such change is necessary (more on this later). In other words, political and policy changes always follow a shift in popular beliefs and values.

Greta Thunberg, an outspoken climate change advocate, expressed this well when she said the following:

I am telling you there is hope. I have seen it. But it does not come from governments or corporations. It comes from the people. The people who have been unaware but are now starting to wake up. And once we become aware, we change.

People can change. People are ready for change. And that is the hope because we have democracy. And democracy is happening all the time, not just on election day, but every second and every hour. It is public opinion that runs the free world. In fact, every great change throughout history has come from the people. We do not have to wait. We can start the change right now.[7]

This is precisely why climate change activists have been so frustrated at the slow progress of governments to react. Governments don't respond until a critical mass of people believe that change is necessary and create significant grassroots momentum for that change. It's not enough to march and demonstrate and grab the day's headlines. This may be part of an organization's attempts to increase awareness and get their message out, but an organization will only be effective in the long run if it succeeds in convincing the masses of the legitimacy and priority of its mission.

The goal is not to convince the government but to convince the people. And this organic and incremental approach to the process of change is where constructive, long-lasting change can be found.

This doesn't mean that Christians should abandon the public square and go back to hiding in their basements and praying that Jesus returns soon. It means we must acknowledge that systemic, lasting change is initiated from shifts in societal beliefs, and then this organic and incremental change is reflected over time in our politics and public policy. Whether we like it or not, shifting the nation takes time.

The successful efforts to promote the changes that I shared in Chapter Three were only possible because the change was preceded by a shift in societal beliefs. This resulted in long-lasting organic and incremental change. Christians who want to change the country by imposing change upon the rest of the population fail to understand that what they're proposing is neither desirable nor possible. It's misguided and dangerous to the stability of civil society and to the health of the church. It will not yield the kind of fruit we want to see.

Change can be promoted at the political level and the public policy level. But we must understand that this kind of change must always be preceded by change at the grassroots level. Only then will the change be constructive and sustainable. Organic and incremental change is the key to shifting the nation.

PART TWO

God's Strategy for Change

GOD WANTS TO shift our nation. But simply changing the government is not the answer. To shift the nation, you must first change the people. And this is what God is in the business of doing.

Change is a popular subject in the Bible. We see it from cover to cover. Things aren't the way they should be, and they need to change. But on our own, the human race is basically helpless when it comes to real change. We can't fix ourselves or better our condition apart from the mercy, grace, and intervention of God. And that's exactly what God did: he intervened to rescue us and make a way so that things could change.

So why is everything still so messed up? If the price for redemption has already been paid in full, why don't we see a greater manifestation of this on the earth? And what—if anything—can we do about it?

The answers to these questions steer us into some pretty intense theological discussions. But if we're going to understand how to shift a nation, we must have a foundational understanding of how God is working on the earth. What, exactly, is his strategy for change? In Part Two, we'll examine this question in detail.

CHAPTER FIVE

We Hold the Keys

ESTHER AND HER people were in trouble. The King of Persia had issued a decree that on a certain day, all of the Jews in the empire were to be annihilated, and this order could not be rescinded. Esther 3:13 details the brutality of what was about to transpire:

> Dispatches were sent by swift messengers into all the provinces of the empire, giving the order that all Jews—young and old, including women and children—must be killed, slaughtered, and annihilated on a single day. This was scheduled to happen on March 7 of the next year. The property of the Jews would be given to those who killed them.

When Esther's cousin, Mordecai, learned about it, he was distraught.

> … he tore his clothes, put on burlap and ashes, and went out into the city, crying with a loud and bitter wail. He went as far as the gate of the palace, for no one was allowed to enter the palace gate while wearing the clothes of mourning. And as news of the king's decree reached all the provinces, there was a

great mourning among the Jews. They fasted, wept, and wailed, and many people lay in burlap and ashes. (Esther 4:1–3)

Queen Esther, on the other hand, was unaware of what was about to take place. Sheltered inside the palace gates, word of the impending tragedy had not yet reached her. So when she was told that Mordecai was at the palace gate dressed in mourning clothes, she was alarmed. Public displays of mourning or distress, such as wearing sackcloth and ashes, were unacceptable in the palace environment. It could be interpreted as a breach of protocol, disrespect to the king and his court, or even a challenge to the existing order. By doing so, Mordecai was placing his life in danger.

Esther responded quickly: "*When Queen Esther's maids and eunuchs came and told her about Mordecai, she was deeply distressed. She sent clothing to him to replace the burlap …*" (Esther 4:4). Because she didn't understand the depth of the problem, Esther tried to fix what was wrong on a superficial level. But Mordecai would have none of it. At the first opportunity, he sent a message to Esther, telling her the whole disturbing story and compelling her to approach the king and beg for mercy for the Jews.

Esther baulked. She was well aware that such an action might cost her life, and she was about to do no such thing. Instead, she sent a message back to Mordecai bluntly pointing this out, saying:

All the king's servants and the people of the king's provinces know that if any man or woman goes to the king inside the inner court without being called, there is but one law—to be put to death, except the one to whom the king holds out the golden scepter so that he may live. But as for me, I have not been called to come in to the king these thirty days." (Esther 4:11, ESV)

Mordecai responded with the following:

> Do not think to yourself that in the king's palace you
> will escape any more than all the other Jews. For if
> you keep silent at this time, relief and deliverance
> will rise for the Jews from another place, but you
> and your father's house will perish. And who knows
> whether you have not come to the kingdom for such
> a time as this? (Esther 4:13b–14, ESV)

Mordecai's message to Esther was clear: "The situation is critical, and you're faced with an unsurpassed opportunity to address it and make an unparalleled impact for good! Opportunity isn't just knocking—it's banging down your door!"

And that's the message we all love to hear: "You were born for such a time as this!" We hear messages like this and we get excited! We all want our lives to matter, and we all want to make a difference! But here's what we tend to miss: *"For if you keep silent at this time, relief and deliverance will rise for the Jews from another place, but you and your father's house will perish."*

Ouch!

Mordecai didn't say, "If you keep quiet at a time like this, no worries; everything will turn out fine because God will raise up someone else to take care of it." He didn't say, "Oh, I know things are bad, but don't worry—God's on the throne." No, he said, "You have been given the opportunity to make a difference. If you choose not to take that opportunity, the cost will be great. Yes, God's purposes will ultimately be fulfilled (at a different time and through someone else), but your inaction will be costly to your life and the lives of many others."

This is a sobering message, and as Christians, we're not accustomed to hearing it. But there it is as plain as day in the biblical story of Esther: we play a critical role in the unfolding purposes of God.

We know that if God wanted to, he could exercise radical, directed change immediately, and in every situation. He could snap his fingers or speak the word and wrongs would be made right, what is broken would be healed, and what is missing would be recovered. In fact, when Christ returns, he will do just that: "*He will wipe away every tear from their eyes, and death shall be no more, neither shall there be mourning, nor crying, nor pain anymore, for the former things have passed away*" (Revelation 21:4, ESV). Everything will be made right one day. But until that day, God is deeply invested in organic, incremental change, which is partly dependent on us and on our response to him.

This can be frustrating. God already holds all the power and knowledge, and he is love. He can fix anything, and he actually wants to. So why doesn't he just unilaterally make more things right instead of taking so long? We're going to delve into this in some detail, but for now we need to understand this: in the kingdom of God, most change is organic and incremental because God has chosen to work through his people and has given us the freedom to choose whether we will do our part.

We can see this clearly on an individual level. If we choose to embrace God's plan and his ways, things begin to come into alignment with the design of his kingdom and restoration takes place over time. As Christians, we have experienced this restoration on a personal level. We may have experienced it in big ways or small ways, but everyone who has received Christ's gift of forgiveness and salvation has a testimony of what God subsequently did in their life to incrementally bring them into greater measures of wholeness.

This pattern repeats over and over in scripture. It's not that there aren't powerful interventions by God that would classify as radical, directed change. Salvation itself is radical, directed change. In a moment, he "*... delivered us from the domain of darkness and transferred us to the kingdom of his beloved Son*" (Colossians 1:13, ESV). Yet even this radical, directed change is contingent on a personal, unforced decision that we make on an individual level. It was not done *to* us … it was done *for* us after we came into agreement with the truth and consented to the intervention of God in our life. It was not imposed on us but was organic change that happened of our own free will as a result of a shift in what we believed. And while the experience itself was radical (it happened in a moment), the journey there is almost always incremental (it takes time).

Changes within societies and nations follow a similar path. Although at times God intervenes to bring about change in a quick and powerful way (consider the great flood, Sodom and Gomorrah, the destruction of Jerusalem in 70 A.D., the cross, the resurrection, etc.), his strategy for change is primarily organic and incremental. We see this reflected in his final instructions to the disciples in Matthew 28:19–20:

> Go therefore and make disciples of all nations, baptizing them in the name of the Father and of the Son and of the Holy Spirit, teaching them to observe all that I have commanded you. And behold, I am with you always, to the end of the age." (ESV)

Acts 1:8 suggests the same organic, incremental approach: "*But you will receive power when the Holy Spirit has come upon you, and you will be my witnesses in Jerusalem and in all Judea and Samaria, and to the end of the earth*" (ESV).

There is widespread agreement amongst theologians that Jesus was instructing the disciples to take an incremental approach to spreading the gospel by beginning in Jerusalem, then moving to Judea and Samaria, and then to the ends of the earth. The kingdom of God would spread throughout the earth gradually and organically through evangelism and discipleship.

This is how the kingdom of God works. On the one hand, it was manifested on the earth through radical, directed change when Jesus became flesh and walked amongst us. On the other hand—as demonstrated by many of Jesus' parables—it is worked out through organic and incremental change. It grows over time. And the extent of that growth depends partly on us.

For some Christians, this will come as a surprise. Much of the church suffers under an illusion of helplessness, where we see ourselves as little more than spectators in the plans and purposes of God. We know that we've been saved, but now we wait either for death or for Christ to return so we can go to heaven. We think this way because this is what we've been taught, but the reality is quite different. Scripture shows us that the children of God are to be the most influential, effective people on earth. What we do actually matters. The church is the salt of society, and when the church loses its saltiness, society rots.

This can be a challenging concept for many Christians, but this is God's design. When it comes to shifting a nation, God doesn't direct events from a distance, just pulling strings from heaven to ensure he gets the outcome he wants. He has chosen to work through people—his people—to impact the destinies of individuals and nations. Rather than being bystanders in the purposes of God, we are called to be partners with him in his work here on the earth.

This means that our personal journey on earth has not been pre-planned. What we do matters and will impact what we accomplish in this life. In spite of the faithfulness of God, the power of God, and the mercy of God, our own welfare and the welfare of others rests partly on the choices we make and the actions we take.

The very mention of this can be alarming and create anxiety and a fear of falling short. But it needs to be understood in its proper context. Salvation is only available through the finished work of Jesus on the cross, yet we know that although Christ paid the price for everyone, not everyone will experience salvation. We all have a responsibility to personally accept this gift. Likewise, much has been provided for us through the cross that we can experience here on earth. But the degree to which we experience this reality is partly contingent on our choices and our faithfulness.

Many people have been told that theirs is a world of opportunity without accountability, that they can have spiritual authority without responsibility. Some have been told that because Jesus paid it all, the work is done and there's nothing left to do. They've been taught a false grace message that says, "Regardless of what you do, everything is going to turn out all right!" Nothing could be further from the truth.

It's true that Jesus did pay it all; salvation is by grace and not by works. But receiving that grace for salvation and appropriating it daily in the challenges and circumstances we face is a responsibility we all carry. How we actively live out our redeemed lives matters.

Ironically, we live in a generation where people are searching for meaning. They're uncertain of their purpose and hungry to know if there's a plan for their life that has value and significance. Yet the mere suggestion that such a discovery might carry with it significant personal responsibility is not always welcomed. While this generation is usually prepared to accept that a failure to steward the environment will impact future generations, they're alarmed by the suggestion that how we live our lives might have an impact on our participation in the plans and purposes of God. But it will.

Esther didn't seem to realize the strategic position she'd been placed in until the time of need. It was then that God sent Mordecai to open her eyes to the opportunity and responsibility that lay before her. She realized that she was holding the keys to the future of her nation. Faced with this reality, Esther's response was to say "yes" to God. She wasn't guaranteed an outcome, but she was given an opportunity, and she said "yes."

In the same way, we hold the keys to the future of our nation. It's not someone else's responsibility—it's ours. We "were born for such a time as this." And we too need to say "yes."

Many Christians believe that the moral decline of society is evidence that we live in the end times. They're convinced that things are predestined to get worse and worse for Christians, culminating in Christ's return. Not only is this not true, but it can cause Christians to resign themselves to believing that nothing can be done, so why try. The church ends up being pessimistic, apathetic, disconnected, and powerless. We complain bitterly about how dark it is, oblivious to the fact that we are the stewards of light.

In the next few chapters, we're going to look at what Christ has chosen to entrust to us. We'll see that because the church holds the keys to bringing a bit of heaven to the earth, we have been given an opportunity to shift the nation and make an impact that will resonate for eternity.

CHAPTER SIX

Understanding the Kingdom of God

IN 1945, WORLD War II was coming to an end. The Japanese Empire had suffered significant losses, and its forces were retreating across various regions. Among those soldiers was a young Japanese man named Hiroo Onoda. Hiroo was stationed on a small island in the Pacific, far away from the mainland.

As the tides of war turned against Japan, Hiroo's unit received orders to retreat. But because of a series of communication breakdowns and chaotic circumstances, Hiroo was left behind on the island. Unaware of the changing events, he continued to hide in the dense jungle, thinking that the war was still ongoing.

Days turned into weeks, and weeks turned into months. Hiroo struggled to survive in the wilderness, relying on his instincts and the limited supplies he could scavenge. He built makeshift shelters, hunted for food, and avoided encounters with other inhabitants of the island.

As time passed, Hiroo's solitude became his reality. He had no contact with the outside world and was cut off from any news or updates regarding the war. He didn't know that the atomic bombs had been dropped on Hiroshima and Nagasaki, leading to Japan's surrender and the subsequent end of the war. He lived in a time capsule, isolated and surviving with the mindset of a soldier who believed he was still fighting a war.

Almost three decades later, in 1974, Hiroo was discovered by a young explorer. Confused and disoriented, Hiroo was initially skeptical of the man's claims that the war had ended. He couldn't fathom the idea that so many years had passed since he'd been left behind. But as more evidence was presented to him, Hiroo's understanding began to shift.

Hiroo Onoda had been living in an alternate reality for years, hiding from the enemy and even conducting occasional raids. He was alive but completely unaware that his perspective and beliefs were not in line with reality. Tragically, he had spent most of his life waiting for something that had already arrived a long time ago.

Today, many Christians live a similar story. They're waiting for Christ to return to establish his kingdom without realizing that the kingdom is already in our midst. As uncomfortable as it may sound, we too can spend our lives waiting for something that is already here. And if we don't understand the present reality of the kingdom we live in, we'll see life pass by, along with the opportunities and adventures that could have been ours. Like the misguided Japanese warrior, our true potential and purpose won't be realized.

If we're going to apprehend the opportunity God has given us and shift the nation, it's imperative to understand that as Christians, we're already part of his kingdom here on the earth. Most of us have heard the words, "kingdom, kingdom of God, kingdom of heaven," but they often mean little to us aside from a fuzzy notion about how God will someday establish his rule when Christ returns. We usually equate it with what things will be like in heaven.

Yet Jesus himself taught his disciples to pray that the kingdom of heaven would come to the *earth*. In parable after parable, Jesus taught his followers the principles of extending the kingdom of God on the earth. Rather than simply waiting for him to return and establish his kingdom, Jesus taught that the kingdom was already in their midst (Luke 17:21) and they had a part to play in its growth.

This lies at the very heart of understanding God's strategy for change on the earth. And for this reason, it's essential that we lay a foundational understanding of the kingdom of God before going further. We're not going to do a comprehensive or exhaustive overview, but we do need to cover four fundamental truths that will help us understand how we can participate more fully in God's strategy for change.

1. The Kingdom of God Is Already Here, but Not in Its Fullness

This first truth is critically important to understand. On the one hand, scripture clearly teaches that God rules over everything. But on the other hand, God is not imposing that rulership on everyone. Psalm 103:19 tells us: *"The Lord has established his throne in the heavens, and his kingdom rules over all"* (ESV).

This truth has never changed. It's a constant, eternal truth. To God belongs all authority, power, and dominion. He is the one with the right to exercise authority. Yet although he has the right and the ability to impose his will and authority on everything, he gives us the choice to respond. John 3:16 illustrates this choice, telling us: *"For God so loved the world, that he gave his only Son, that whoever believes in him should not perish but have eternal life"* (ESV).

Although God is the rightful ruler, and he reigns everywhere, he has chosen to temporarily limit the exercise of his rule to those who voluntarily choose to come under it. Although he holds all authority, he has chosen to share that authority with a people who, out of love, choose to surrender to Him. This means his kingdom is present on the earth where people have made this voluntary decision to come under his authority.

This understanding is foundational, and it's not controversial amongst Evangelical Christians. While nuances exist, it's generally embraced but often not taught as clearly or frequently as it should be. Regrettably, this leaves many Christians with the impression that we're waiting for the kingdom of God to come to earth. In reality, it's already here, though not in its fullness, because God is not imposing it on people.

2. The Kingdom of God Is Not Political

In Jesus' day, the coming of the kingdom of God to the earth was highly anticipated by the Jews. They were anxiously waiting for it. But they expected a political kingdom in which the Messiah would overthrow the Romans, establish himself as the political king of Israel, and inaugurate God's government. They pictured it like it was in the days of King David. And for good reason. This imagery was used by Old Testament prophets when they spoke of the coming Messiah. But what they didn't recognize was that this kingdom would first be a kingdom of the heart. It wouldn't be won by force, coercion, and war but by winning the hearts of people through love, mercy, and forgiveness.

When speaking of shifting the nation, it's critical to remember this. The role of the church is not to take over and force non-Christians to act like they're followers of Christ. The role of the church is to represent Christ and permeate society like leaven with love, joy, peace, hope, kindness, wisdom, healing, deliverance, provision, and more. We aren't to impose something on people that they don't want, but we're to follow the example of Jesus and bring light and life to every corner of society and aspect of life.

The fact that the kingdom of God isn't the political kingdom the Jews were expecting makes it no less real. It was heralded by John the Baptist and declared to be present by Jesus himself: *"Jesus traveled throughout the region of Galilee, teaching in the synagogues and announcing the Good News about the Kingdom. And he healed every kind of disease and illness"* (Matthew 4:23). Later, Jesus told the Pharisees that, *"...if I am casting out demons by the Spirit of God, then the kingdom of God has arrived among you"* (Matthew 12:28).

There was no doubt that the kingdom of God had arrived on the earth. It came with Jesus, and it's here now for those who will receive it. It's the rule of the King that reconnects us with our maker and brings an extension of a bit of heaven on the earth, displacing darkness, despair, brokenness, and strife.

3. We Can Live in the Kingdom of God

The good news is that if we choose to, we can enter the kingdom of God. We can become subjects in God's kingdom right now. But to do so, we must enter the kingdom according to the terms of the king.

Some people teach that there are many ways to God. This is not true. Christ taught that there was only one way—through Him. We don't get to enter the kingdom of God because we're good enough, gifted enough, humble enough, or smart enough. We enter the kingdom of God when we accept by faith what Christ did for us through his death and resurrection.

Some people think that we don't enter the kingdom of God until we die and go to heaven, but again, scripture makes it clear that we enter God's kingdom while we're here on earth. We saw this earlier in Colossians 1:13–14: *"For he has rescued us from the kingdom of darkness and transferred us into the Kingdom of his dear Son, who purchased our freedom and forgave our sins."* Note that it says he *"rescued"* us and *"transferred"* us, not that he rescued us and will one day transfer us into *"the Kingdom of his dear Son."* Both verbs are past tense, which means that Christians are already part of the kingdom of God.

In Acts 26, Paul recounts the story of his salvation and tells us that Jesus said this to him:

> But get up and stand on your feet; for this purpose I
> have appeared to you, to appoint you a minister and
> a witness not only to the things which you have seen,
> but also to the things in which I will appear to you;
> rescuing you from the Jewish people and from the

> Gentiles, to whom I am sending you, to open their
> eyes *so that they may turn from darkness to light and
> from the dominion of Satan to God*, that they may
> receive forgiveness of sins and an inheritance among
> those who have been sanctified by faith in Me." (Acts
> 26:16–18, NASB 1995, emphasis added)

When we give our lives to God, we come out from under the
authority of the devil and come under the authority of Jesus. In other
words, we go from the dominion of Satan to the dominion, or the
kingdom, of God. This means that when we become the children of
God, we live under the authority of the King. At that point, Satan no
longer has any rightful authority over us. None. We have chosen to
become subjects of the King, and wherever the King rules, there is
love, peace, joy, hope, sufficiency, and wholeness.

This doesn't mean that Christians are exempt from difficulties
and hardship; it means that the antidote to the brokenness of humanity and society is found in the kingdom of God, where we now reside.
By entering and learning to live as citizens of his kingdom, we find
not only that our lives come into increasing wholeness, but we're able
to help others find wholeness as well and see that wholeness begin to
permeate throughout society.

4. The Kingdom of God Is Growing

The kingdom of God doesn't diminish in size or impact. Scripture
tells us that the kingdom of God has only increased since Jesus
came, and it will only continue to increase. Isaiah 9:6–7 reads:

> For a child will be born to us, a son will be given to
> us; and the government will rest on his shoulders;
> and his name will be called Wonderful Counselor,
> Mighty God, Eternal Father, Prince of Peace. There
> will be no end to the increase of His government or
> of peace, on the throne of David and over his king-

dom, to establish it and to uphold it with justice and righteousness from then on and forevermore. The zeal of the Lord of hosts will accomplish this. (NASB 1995)

"There will be no end to the increase of his government." This clearly contradicts the idea that the church was at its best in the book of Acts, and that things are basically going to get worse and worse until Jesus comes and rescues his people just before they're all obliterated. On the contrary, it indicates that anything that is not consistent with the will of the King is passing away. We see this truth illustrated in Daniel 7:13–14:

> As my vision continued that night, I saw someone like a son of man coming with the clouds of heaven. He approached the Ancient One and was led into his presence. He was given authority, honor, and sovereignty over all the nations of the world, so that people of every race and nation and language would obey him. His rule is eternal—it will never end. His kingdom will never be destroyed. (Daniel 7:13–14)

Many Christians understand this passage to be referring to the return of Christ, but it more closely depicts what happened at Christ's ascension. We'll look at this more closely in the next chapter, but for now it establishes once again that the kingdom of God is eternal. It will never end, and it will never be destroyed. In fact, it is always increasing.

Jesus told this to his disciples in the parable of the mustard seed:

> With what can we compare the kingdom of God, or what parable shall we use for it? It is like a grain of mustard seed, which, when sown on the ground, is the smallest of all the seeds on earth, yet when it is

> sown it grows up and becomes larger than all the garden plants and puts out large branches, so that the birds of the air can make nests in its shade. (Mark 4:30–32, ESV)

The kingdom of God will start small and grow, Jesus explained. Like a mustard seed, it will sprout and continually get larger and larger. It will only increase.

Paul echoes this sentiment in his letter to the Colossians: "*... the gospel which has come to you, just as in all the world also it is constantly bearing fruit and increasing ...*" (Colossians 1:5b, 6a, NASB 1995). Paul saw the impact and effect of the gospel as "*constantly bearing fruit and increasing.*" He was participating in a kingdom that was increasing, not struggling to survive and barely getting by.

In order to understand the responsibility and opportunity God has given us and to shift the nation, we must first understand these four things about the kingdom of God: The kingdom of God is already here but not in its fullness; the kingdom of God is not political; we can live in that kingdom now; and the kingdom of God is growing. This is a biblical perspective of the kingdom of God, and understanding it begins to open up an awareness of God's strategy for change and our place in it!

CHAPTER SEVEN

Understanding the Authority of Christ

HAVING GOTTEN THIS far, we face a common and important question: "If God is all-powerful, then why does he allow evil in the world? Why would a good God allow innocent people to be harmed? Either he's not all-powerful, or he's not a good God, because this makes no sense!"

This question is relevant when we're considering how to shift the nation. Is the nation in the condition it is because of God's will? And if not, how is that even possible, since he is all-powerful?

In order to properly understand these things, we must understand the authority of Christ.

All Authority Has Been Given to Jesus

In Matthew 28:18, Jesus makes a clear statement to his disciples: "I have been given all authority in heaven and on earth." We don't know if this shocked his disciples or if they even understood the significance of it at the time, but the meaning of the statement was clear: Jesus had been given all authority in heaven and on earth. He didn't say that someday he would receive all authority, or that he had received some authority. He said he had been given it all, and that it belonged to him right now. Scripture repeats this fact over and over:

> ... God elevated him to the place of highest honor and gave him the name above all other names, that at the name of Jesus every knee should bow, in heaven and on earth and under the earth, and every tongue declare that Jesus Christ is Lord, to the glory of God the Father. (Philippians 2:9–11)

> God has put all things under the authority of Christ and has made him head over all things for the benefit of the church. (Ephesians 1:22)

This simple truth is accepted by Christians today. We hear it repeated in songs and declared in teachings. Jesus holds all authority in heaven and on earth; he is the King of Kings and Lord of Lords.

But for most of us, this belief is problematic, because from our vantage point, Jesus doesn't act like someone who has all authority. In fact, he seems kind of passive. I mean, if Jesus has been given all authority, why does he allow so many bad things to happen in the world? And if all authority belongs to him, why doesn't he use it to rid the world of evil? Or at least protect the innocent? We may hear the occasional story where someone claims that God intervened and radically rescued their life, but in most people's lives, these stories are rare. Instead, this all-powerful God seems to stand idly by while the world goes from bad to worse. Violence, suicides, tragedies, abuse—these things invade the evening news and creep into our lives. We're left to quietly conclude that either Jesus doesn't actually have all authority, or he's choosing not to use it for some inexplicable reason.

Many people have been embittered against God their entire lives because when tragedy struck, they were told that "God allowed it." Yet they, being much less righteous than God, couldn't fathom being in a position to prevent tragedy and doing nothing about it. How could a God who holds all power and authority be so passive and distant if he's so strong, loving, and good? These are difficult questions. But when we wrestle with how to shift the nation toward a greater degree of wholeness, we need to grapple with them. Our answers and understanding have a significant bearing on what we believe can be done and our role in getting it done. Understanding that Jesus holds all authority is the beginning of our journey to making sense out of all this.

Christ Received His Authority after His Ascension

Christ's authority was given to him by the Father after his ascension to the Father. Consider the following scriptures:

> ...he humbled himself in obedience to God and died a criminal's death on a cross. Therefore, God elevated him to the place of highest honor and gave him the name above all other names, that at the name of Jesus every knee should bow, in heaven and on earth and under the earth, and every tongue declare that Jesus Christ is Lord, to the glory of God the Father. (Philippians 2:8–11)

> This is the same mighty power that raised Christ from the dead and seated him in the place of honor at God's right hand in the heavenly realms. Now he is far above any ruler or authority or power or leader or anything else—not only in this world but also in the world to come. God has put all things under the authority of Christ and has made him head over all things for the benefit of the church. (Ephesians 1:19b–22)

> But our High Priest offered himself to God as a single sacrifice for sins, good for all time. Then he sat

TO SHIFT A NATION

down in the place of honor at God's right hand. (Hebrews 10:12)

> The Lord said to my Lord, "Sit in the place of honor
> at my right hand until I humble your enemies, mak-
> ing them a footstool under your feet." The Lord will
> extend your powerful kingdom from Jerusalem; you
> will rule over your enemies. (Psalm 110:1–2)

This is a significant theme throughout the Bible. In fact, Psalm
110:1–2 is referred to more often in the New Testament than any other Old Testament passage. Obviously, this truth is important, if not
central, to the purposes of God.

From these scriptures, the picture is clear: Christ, having paid
the price of redemption, was raised from the dead and ascended to
his Father, at which time the Father bestowed on him all authority. Jesus announces this to the disciples in Matthew 28:18b: "*I have
been given all authority in heaven and on earth.*" Jesus was alluding to
Daniel 7, where Daniel was allowed to peer into the future and watch
the event unfold:

> As my vision continued that night, I saw someone
> like a son of man coming with the clouds of heav-
> en. He approached the Ancient One and was led into
> his presence. He was given authority, honor, and
> sovereignty over all the nations of the world, so that
> people of every race and nation and language would
> obey him. His rule is eternal—it will never end. His
> kingdom will never be destroyed. (Daniel 7:13–14)

His disciples would have been familiar with this scripture and
would have recognized that Jesus was clearly claiming to be the fulfilment of this passage. When he ascended to the Father after the

resurrection, he received all authority, honour, and sovereignty over all the nations of the world, and his rule would never end.

But there's more.

All Things Are Not Yet Subject to Christ's Authority

Many teachings stop with the previous point, without moving on to the next critical one: Although all authority has been given to Christ, all of his enemies have not yet been subjected to his authority. If you've never heard this before, it might come as a bit of a shock. But this too is very clear in scripture. Consider what these verses tell us:

> The Lord says to my Lord: "Sit at My right hand until I make Your enemies a footstool for Your feet." The Lord will stretch forth Your strong scepter from Zion, saying, "Rule in the midst of Your enemies." (Psalm 110:1–2, NASB)

> But our High Priest offered himself to God as a single sacrifice for sins, good for all time. Then he sat down in the place of honor at God's right hand. There he waits until his enemies are humbled and made a footstool under his feet. (Hebrews 10:12–13)

> For Christ must reign until he humbles all his enemies beneath his feet. (1 Corinthians 15:25)

It couldn't be any clearer, but we're not used to hearing it: Although all authority has been given to Jesus, the *full* exercise of that authority is not yet in effect. All of his enemies are not currently being subjected to his authority.

This might take a minute to digest, but when you think about it, it makes sense and explains a lot. Christ's authority is real, and it was immediate. But the enactment or exercise or enforcement of that authority takes place *over a period of time*. In Colossians 1:18, the apostle Paul alludes to this: *"He is also head of the body, the church; and He is the beginning, the firstborn from the dead, so that He Himself might come to have first place in everything"* (NASB). Jesus is already head of the church, the beginning, and the firstborn from the dead, yet he doesn't yet have first place in everything. Rather, this will happen over time. He will *"come to have first place in everything."*

If we get this wrong, we get many things wrong. We begin to blame God for things he has nothing to do with. We begin to think things are his will just because they happen, even if they don't line up with what we see in scripture. This yields nothing but confusion and disillusionment.

We should be encouraged that we're not alone in this misunderstanding, as it was even shared by Jesus' disciples. They thought Jesus was going to establish his kingdom in one big bang, overturning the Romans and giving power back to the Jewish people. The closer Jesus got to Jerusalem, the more the disciples seemed to anticipate that this event was just around the corner. Jesus knew that he needed to correct this misunderstanding, so he told them the parable of the ten servants:

> As they heard these things, he [Jesus] proceeded to tell a parable, because he was near to Jerusalem, and because they supposed that the kingdom of God was to appear immediately. He said therefore, "A nobleman went into a far country to receive for himself a kingdom and then return. Calling ten of his servants, he gave them ten minas, and said to them, 'Engage in business until I come.' But his citizens hated him and sent a delegation after him, saying, 'We do not want this man to reign over us.' When he returned, having received the kingdom, he ordered these servants to whom he had given the money to be called

to him, that he might know what they had gained by doing business." (Luke 19:11–15, ESV)

Jesus' message wasn't that the kingdom had not arrived—he had already made it quite clear that it had. Rather, the message was that the kingdom had not yet arrived in its fullness and would not for some time. There would be a gap between when he received the kingdom and when he returned to impose his absolute rule as the rightful King.

This illustration would have been very familiar to his listeners. In 40 B.C., Herod the Great had to go to Rome to receive the right to rule Judea. When he returned, he had to fight for another three years to secure his control of the kingdom, because the people didn't want him as their ruler. Similarly, when his son Archelaus went to Rome to be crowned, the people sent a representation of fifty people to Rome after him to oppose his appointment. Jesus used a well-known bit of contemporary history to convey an important truth to his disciples.

We see another picture of this when David became king over Judah. Although he had been anointed by God as king over all of Israel, he met opposition. He had been duly granted the authority, but not everyone was yet subject to that authority: "*That was the beginning of a long war between those who were loyal to Saul and those loyal to David. As time passed David became stronger and stronger, while Saul's dynasty became weaker and weaker*" (2 Samuel 3:1). This passage serves as an excellent illustration of the season the church finds itself in today. Christ has all authority, but everything is not yet subject to his authority. The kingdom of God is becoming stronger and stronger, and the kingdom of darkness is growing weaker and weaker.

There is a day coming when all things will be subject to Christ's authority. But for now, we have the choice of whether we'll come under that authority or not. The day when all things are subjected to Christ is the day when that opportunity to choose will be over.

Jesus Is Returning to Place All His Enemies under His Feet

This brings us to the next key point: Jesus is returning to bring to completion the process of seeing all his enemies put under his feet. Most of us have been taught that everything will be put under Christ's feet in one gigantic blow when he returns. But this is not what scripture indicates.

Speaking of the resurrection at the end of the age, Paul writes:

> But there is an order to this resurrection: Christ was raised as the first of the harvest; then all who belong to Christ will be raised when he comes back. After that the end will come, when he will turn the Kingdom over to God the Father, having destroyed every ruler and authority and power. For Christ must reign until he humbles all his enemies beneath his feet. And the last enemy to be destroyed is death … Then, when all things are under his authority, the Son will put himself under God's authority, so that God, who gave his Son authority over all things, will be utterly supreme over everything everywhere. (1 Corinthians 15:23–26, 28)

Let's unpack this a bit. The sequence begins with Christ being raised from the dead. He is given all authority and begins his reign, which will last until he humbles all his enemies beneath his feet. The very last enemy to be destroyed will be death, which takes place when Christ returns and all who belong to him are raised from the dead. Once this happens, and all his enemies are under his feet, Christ will put himself under God's authority so that God will be utterly supreme over everything everywhere.

Here's the part we need to pay attention to: The *last* enemy to be destroyed is death. This suggests that before death is destroyed, his other enemies are already being humbled beneath his feet. This is significant because it takes us right back to Isaiah 9:7, which says, *"There will be no end to the increase of His government ..."* With no end to the increase of his government, it means that between the ascension and his return, his government (his kingdom) is continually increasing!

This might be hard to get our heads around, but we really need to absorb it. Every day, the enemy—Satan—loses a little more ground. Every day, the kingdom of God is increasing, which means the kingdom of darkness is decreasing. Every day, the devil finds himself with a smaller and smaller domain as the dominion of God expands.

There's a great verse in Daniel that illustrates this: *"But the court shall sit in judgment, and his dominion shall be taken away, to be consumed and destroyed to the end"* (Daniel 7:26, ESV). Although we won't get into whether or not this verse literally refers to Satan and his dominion of darkness, it's an excellent illustration of what was and is taking place. Through the death and resurrection of Christ, Satan's dominion was *"taken away"* and is now being *"consumed and destroyed to the end."* In other words, it may take a while, but the kingdom of God is increasing at the expense of the kingdom of darkness!

All of this will one day culminate in what Paul describes in Ephesians 1:9–10:

> God has now revealed to us his mysterious will regarding Christ—which is to fulfill his own good plan. And this is the plan: At the right time he will bring everything together under the authority of Christ—everything in heaven and on earth.

The day is coming when *everything* will be under the authority of Christ. And until that day, we are not just barely holding on—we are part of the team that is taking ground while the other side is losing ground![8]

CHAPTER EIGHT

Understanding Our Authority

SO HOW DOES this work and what is our role? Are we mere bystanders as Christ works to bring all things into subjection to his authority? Do we have a part to play? If so, what is it? The answers to these questions are critical when considering how to shift a nation, and they begin with four important truths that we need to understand.

1. God Doesn't Work Alone

When it comes to understanding our role in the advancement of the kingdom of God on the earth and the gradual subjection of all things to his authority, we need to understand that God doesn't work alone. He has never worked alone. Even in eternity past, the Father, Son, and Holy Spirit worked in concert and agreement with one another.

With the creation of mankind, this heart of partnership continued. A covenant relationship was established between God and man, where God chose to partner with his people in his work on the earth. Although God is entirely capable of just doing it all himself, he chose to work with us and through us.

This truth emerges constantly throughout scripture, in both the Old and New Testaments. In fact, it's difficult to find a Bible story that doesn't convey this truth: the promise of a son to Abraham required his faith and obedience. The promised land was taken through a series of battles, not simply handed over to the Israelites, and the welfare of the nation of Israel was contingent on how the leaders and the people responded to God. The examples go on and on.

It's not that God needs our help; it's that he has chosen to work this way. His desire is for a family that operates within a kingdom under the direction of our Father the King.

2. What We Do Matters

When you begin to see this principle, you start to notice it everywhere in scripture: we are in partnership with God, and what we do matters. The final outcome is guaranteed. God is establishing his kingdom on the earth, and he will rule forever. But the extent of our participation in that process isn't guaranteed. It's dependent on our choices and our actions.

Consider this well-known passage. Here Jesus makes an astounding statement when he tells his disciples, "*The harvest is great, but the workers are few. So pray to the Lord who is in charge of the harvest; ask him to send more workers into his fields*" (Matthew 9:37–38).

Most of us have heard or read this scripture many times. We're familiar with the challenge to be active in the harvest field, but we may have missed something very profound: this suggests that the Lord of the harvest is unprepared for the harvest!

This is highly unusual, since no capable farmer would ever find himself in such a position. A farmer knows well in advance if his crop is going to be plentiful, and the necessary preparations are made long before harvest time arrives. As the crop grows and matures, its size is evident, and the yield can be closely estimated. The farmer goes to work to prepare for it. If necessary, new storage bins are built, temporary workers are hired, and additional machinery is acquired. Whatever is needed is secured well in advance so that everything is in place when harvest season arrives and the crop isn't left to spoil in the field.

Yet here we have a picture of a great harvest and not enough workers to bring it in. How is it possible that the Lord of the harvest would be unprepared for the harvest? It can only mean one thing: the Lord of the harvest delegated a degree of responsibility to others.

When Jesus shares this with the disciples, we don't see him scold them, or even correct them. He uses a very teachable moment to share something profound: the advancement of the kingdom of God depends in part on the people of God.

While we often hear about this passage in terms of evangelism and salvation, that's only part of the picture. The admonition has a clear application to not just salvation, but also to healing, deliverance, and everything provided to us through the cross. It was given in the context of Jesus sending out seventy-two disciples to visit all the towns and places he planned to visit. Their instructions were clear: "*Heal the sick, raise the dead, cure those with leprosy, and cast out demons. Give as freely as you have received!*" (Matthew 10:8).

In this context, Jesus said, "*The harvest is great, but the workers are few*" (Matthew 9:37). In other words, there is no shortage of healing, deliverance, or salvation. The problem is not with supply but with the availability of workers who know how to access and minister out of what has been provided.

There is a popular misconception that God has everything under control, and if he wants something to happen, it will happen. Yet these verses and many others suggest otherwise. We will examine this further in later chapters, but suffice it to say that God has limited his "control" because he has chosen to share a measure of that control with us.

Our God does not work alone, and some of what happens, or doesn't happen, depends on us. This doesn't change the inevitability of the final outcome, but it does present a large door of opportunity for us to partner with God in the increase of his kingdom on the earth.

3. God Uses the Church to Subdue His Enemies

Scripture teaches us that Christ uses his Church to subdue his enemies and participate in bringing all things under his authority. He doesn't just sit in heaven and wave his sceptre and then everything falls into proper alignment with his authority. It's actually much more beautiful and relational and honouring than that: the authority that belongs to Christ as the head is exercised on the earth through his body, the Church.

> One day Jesus called together his twelve disciples and gave them power and authority to cast out demons and to heal all diseases. Then he sent them out to tell everyone about the Kingdom of God and to heal the sick ... So they began their circuit of the villages, preaching the Good News and healing the sick. (Luke 9:1–2, 6)

Jesus gave his disciples power and authority. Power is just that—the power of God (*dunamis*)—and authority is the right to use God's power. He gives power and authority to his disciples and sends them out.

Note what they do: They don't repeatedly phone home for the next few days and say, "Jesus, so-and-so wants to be healed. Do you want him to be healed? Jesus, so-and-so needs deliverance, is it your will to free him?" Instead, having been given power and authority, they simply stepped out in faith and proceeded to fulfil the mandate given to them by Jesus.

In fact, before the disciples went out, one of Jesus' instructions to them was, "*Give as freely as you have received*" (Matthew 10:8b). The NASB version translates it this way: "*Freely you have received, freely give.*" They weren't told to cautiously and carefully vet every person's worth or spiritual condition before they proceeded to minister healing and deliverance. They were told to pour it out as freely as they had received.

Jesus essentially told them, "Look, you're carrying something on my behalf, and you have a critical role in distributing it. The degree to which you release it is the degree to which it will be shared with others."

4. The Extension of the Kingdom Is Intentional, Not Accidental or Incidental

A better translation of *"Give as freely as you have received"* would be, "Bestow as freely as you have obtained." The word "received" in the Greek is *lambano*, which means to "get hold of." It is in the active voice. If it was in the passive voice, it would mean "to have offered to one." In the active voice it's not a picture of someone putting their hands out to receive something but of someone laying hold of something and not letting go. They "obtained" it; they didn't sit back and wait for it to arrive.

"Give" is also in the active voice. From the Greek word *didomi*, it can even mean to strike or to smite. There's nothing passive about it. It didn't mean to offer but rather to *bestow*. It's an intentional impartation delivered with authority. The disciples were instructed that in the same way they seized the things of the kingdom, they were to intentionally and authoritatively impart them as well.

At another time, Jesus said to the disciples, *"... the kingdom of heaven suffereth violence, and the violent take it by force."* (Matthew 11:12b, KJV). Although the meaning of this verse has been debated endlessly, a plain reading of it tells us a lot: the kingdom of heaven can be apprehended, but it requires some deliberate action on our part.

The word "violent" means "to apply force." It doesn't indicate that people are being hurt but that they are actively and intentionally laying hold of the kingdom of God. Most people think that to receive something from heaven you just pray, hope, and wait. While that may be true sometimes, at other times we must apprehend the things of heaven. This is where the *"violent"* take it by force. It involves the exercise of authority.

This truth is repeated over and over in scripture. We see it again when Jesus says, "*I will give you the keys of the kingdom of heaven; and whatever you bind on earth shall have been bound in heaven, and whatever you loose on earth shall have been loosed in heaven*" (Matthew 16:19, NASB). We have been entrusted with the authority to bind hell on earth and to release heaven on earth. We can glean a lot from this, but at the most basic level, it underscores the fact that everything is not up to God.

One incident constantly reminds me of this truth. It happened quite a few years ago but is still fresh in my mind. My wife and I were meeting my mom and dad for breakfast at a restaurant. When we arrived, they were already seated at a table, across from each other. Gail sat down next to my dad, and I sat beside my mom.

It was then that I noticed her wrist wrapped in a brace. I asked her about it, and she explained that she'd been experiencing increasing pain due to tendonitis in her right thumb. It had been bothering her for some months and then got a lot worse after she caught her thumb on something and bent it back. The doctor told her not to use that hand until it was completely healed and to come see him so she could be fitted with a splint.

When my mom finished describing what was wrong, I gently placed my hand on her wrist and said the word, "Healing!" It was the shortest prayer I had ever prayed, but I could feel the compassion and the presence of God quite strongly in that moment. I felt like something had happened and considered asking her to take her wrist brace off to check if there was any change in the condition but decided against it. However, the next day when my mom got up, she noticed that there was no pain and tried using it a bit. There was still no pain, so she tried putting more pressure on it. The pain was completely gone.

Later that day my mom went to her appointment to be fitted for the splint. After checking it out, the doctor asked, "What happened? Your thumb and wrist look fine!" She had been completely healed through a very simple prayer.

My mom was healed by the Spirit of God, but it didn't happen until I prayed for her. Had I not released healing through prayer, that healing would not have taken place. That's not to say that perhaps she wouldn't have been healed through someone else's prayers at a different time, but the healing was released in that moment because I responded to the prompting of the Spirit of God in prayer.

God's strategy for change isn't just to act unilaterally and force everything into line with his will and purposes. He has chosen instead to partner with us. This means that we have an important role to play in extending the kingdom of God on the earth. We're not to sit back and wait for God to do everything on our behalf. Power and authority have been given to the Church to be exercised generously under divine direction and in accordance with divine purposes. We are critical in God's plan to shift the nation.

CHAPTER NINE

Participating in the Kingdom

IF WE'RE WAITING for some spiritual or political superstar to arise and shift the nation, we are sadly mistaken. God's strategy for change involves everyday men and women through whom he can work to bring a bit of heaven to earth, rescue the broken, and bring the nation into greater measures of wholeness—one person, family, and community at a time. This requires people who know God, love God, and regularly experience the reality of the kingdom of God in and through their lives.

As Christians, we often allow our experience to determine our theology rather than allowing our theology to determine our experience. So if we're not experiencing the kingdom of God like the disciples did, or like Jesus said we should, we simply alter our theology accordingly. This ends up significantly limiting our impact.

We pray for people and don't see them all get healed, so we develop a theology that says, "God doesn't want everyone healed." Because some churches don't see the gifts of the Spirit active in their lives, they adopt a theology that says the gifts of the Spirit passed away with the passing of the disciples. Others have never seen a true miracle, so they insist that miracles were only necessary to establish the Church in the book of Acts. The examples could go on and on, but you get the point. If we're not careful, we will try to conform the Word of God to our experience, instead of insisting that our experience conform to the Word of God.

There may be many reasons why our experience doesn't always line up with the Word of God, but the fact that it doesn't highlights one significant truth: Walking in the reality of the kingdom is neither automatic nor guaranteed. Some of it depends on us.

It's possible to be a Christian yet miss out on the fruitfulness and effectiveness that is available, or on the peace and joy that are part of the kingdom. It's possible that even though they're available to us, we may never see a miracle or a healing or a deliverance. We could go through our entire Christian life and never experience the things that are available to us in the kingdom or operate in the level of anointing and authority that awaits us.

This can be difficult to hear. It's easier to assume that if God wants someone healed, then he will heal them. Or if God wants someone delivered, he will deliver them. It takes some courage to accept responsibility on our part if we're going to participate in the kingdom like God wants us to and see the nation shift.

So the obvious questions are: What does scripture teach us about walking in the reality of the kingdom of God? What will enable us to experience more of heaven on earth? To answer these, we need to consider three things: our Father, our opportunity, and our responsibility.

UNDERSTANDING OUR FATHER

Our journey to experience more of heaven on earth begins here: understanding the heart of our heavenly Father. There's something in each of us that struggles against intimacy with God. We sometimes (or perhaps often) see ourselves as distant from God and in need of proving ourselves to him. We view others as closer to God and perhaps even more favoured by him. This may not even be a conscious posture, but it's often one we've learned or adopted over time because we don't understand the Father's heart for us.

"Let us therefore come boldly unto the throne of grace, that we may obtain mercy, and find grace to help in time of need" (Hebrews 4:16, KJV). We read scriptures like this, yet we don't feel bold about coming to the throne of grace. We remember our shortcomings, our past failures, our disappointments, and our unfulfilled dreams. We tend to view the Father through the lens of our own track record rather than embracing what he has said about us. We believe he wants to use others, but we're not so sure he wants to use us.

This is perhaps one of the greatest limitations to walking in the reality of the life God wants us to experience. Rather than drawing near boldly with expectation, we hang back. We struggle with being too confident in our relationship with God because it feels pretentious or prideful. After all, we know we're not perfect.

For some people, this reluctance may be rooted in an experience of believing God for a breakthrough that never came. Perhaps we were confident that a certain situation was going to turn out differently than it did. Perhaps tragedy struck us or a loved one unexpectedly. These things can create uncertainty and confusion that linger like a hazy fog—almost unnoticeable but still obscuring our vision of the Father. Even though we may not be consciously thinking about these memories, they can cause us to be hesitant in our faith rather than confident in the heart of our Father.

God wants to break off any uncertainty we may have in his goodness. He has powerful things that he wants to do in us and through us, but he needs us to see ourselves as he sees us. So how does God view us? Scripture is infused with messages of God's heart for us, but consider what this familiar passage tells us:

> For God so loved the world that he gave his only Son, that whoever believes in him should not perish but have eternal life. For God did not send his Son into the world to condemn the world, but in order

that the world might be saved through him. (John 3:16–17, ESV)

This is likely the most-quoted portion of the Bible, next to Psalm 23. Perhaps because of that, we hear it but miss the depth and strength of what it's saying about how God views us. These two verses give us six powerful truths that we need to let soak deep into our hearts and change us.

1. God Is for You

"For God so loved the world."

The first truth is that God is for you. We sometimes think of God as being a bit temperamental, especially when we read the Old Testament without understanding what's going on. We may think God is aloof and measuring us from a distance, only occasionally drawing near unexpectedly.

But God is not against you, he is not distant from you, and he is not ambivalent about you. He's not measuring your every move waiting for you to mess up. He won't reject you, mislead you, or fail you. He's committed to your success and your wellbeing. God views you as a loving parent views a growing child: not perfect, but adorable. He doesn't deny that we have flaws, but he's confident in his ability to iron out those wrinkles as we walk with him. And he's not just fixated on the destination—he actually loves the journey! He enjoys walking with us as we grow to be more like him and come to know him more intimately.

Depending on our history, these truths can be hard to absorb. If we've experienced situations or been in relationships where trust has been broken, or people have been unreliable, we can develop a pattern of not relying on anyone other than ourselves. We may keep a "healthy" distance from others in order to protect ourselves from being hurt again.

But whether we realize it or not, this tendency will spill over into our relationship with God. We know that God is faithful, yet the baggage of our past (or present) hinders us from really absorbing this truth. We paint our relationship with God with the same brush that paints our understanding of the relationships around us. But God wants to break that off of us as we meditate on his Word and spend time in his presence.

Other people struggle under the burden of performance. They feel that nothing they do is quite good enough for God, and that although God loves them, they will never measure up to his expectations. Although they come to him in prayer and worship and even experience his presence, a blanket of rejection dulls their hearts and minds, causing them to be hesitant when they approach him.

These presets can be rooted in our relationship with our parents when we were growing up or in other interactions that left us with a sense of inadequacy. But sometimes it's simply a reflection of the fact that we've never really accepted our complete inability to pay for our salvation. Paul had to exhort the New Testament believers over and over to not go back to trying to earn their salvation through their works. For some reason we all tend to fall into this trap, and we need to consciously return to the fact that God not only loves us, but he loved us first! He loved us even while we were his enemies, so why on earth would he be hesitant in his love toward us now that we're trying to follow him faithfully?

God is not hesitant in his love toward us. As difficult as we may find it to comprehend, his love is selfless and generous, unconditional and never wavering. We need to let this sink deep into our souls, because if we begin to see it, it will transform how we view God and light a fire within us that burns with expectation that he wants to work with us and through us to repair a broken world.

2. God Will Go to Any Length for Your Benefit

"For God so loved the world that he gave his only Son."

God not only loves you but he gave away what was most precious to him for you. The Father paid the ultimate price by sending his Son, Jesus, to walk amongst us and die a brutal death for our salvation.

We sometimes minimize that cost by thinking, *Well, God knew that Jesus was going to rise from the dead, so it wasn't really that big of a deal.* But which one of us wouldn't struggle to allow one of our children to go through an unbearably painful experience, even if we knew that they were going to come out the other end of it? If such a thing was avoidable, we'd do everything within our power to ensure that our child didn't go through that experience. Unless the reward of the suffering was far greater than the price.

This is how the Father views us. He places such value on us that he was willing to do the unthinkable in order to restore us to relationship with him. And having done that, he'll stop at nothing to try to reach you, bless you, or bring you into fullness of life in him.

In Romans 8:32, Paul says, *"He who did not spare his own Son, but delivered Him up for us all, how will He not also with Him freely give us all things?"* (NASB). In other words, since he was willing to pay the highest possible price for our salvation, he's not going to hesitate to ensure we have access to it.

The truth is, we find this hard to believe. We hear the words, but we don't feel the strength of them. And because we don't believe, we have trouble accepting that God would do these things for us. We think that we're the exception to the rule, so we wrestle with God instead of just accepting what he has said as true.

We need to understand that faith is not having confidence in our faith—it's being convinced that God is faithful (Hebrews 11:11). It's deciding that regardless of how we feel, God is faithful. When the uncertainty rages inside our heads and hearts, we don't need to try to silence it all. We just need to choose to take God's side by reminding ourselves that ultimately what he says is true.

God loves you and is willing to go to any length for your benefit. If it doesn't feel like that now, just accept this truth and start to admit it out loud. As you do, your feelings will begin to come into alignment with the truth. You've not been left to struggle, trying to figure this life out on your own and just make the best of it. He has provided much more for you!

3. God Paid Everything to Rescue You and Rewrite Your Story

> *"For God so loved the world that he gave his only Son,* _that whoever believes in him should not perish_*"* (emphasis added).

Before God intervened, we were all destined for destruction. No other paths were available to us, no matter how good we were or how hard we tried. We were on a road we could not get off. But God would have none of it. He wasn't willing to see his creation end that way. He had a different ending in mind. So he stepped in and rescued us by paying the price in full: *"but He, having offered one sacrifice for sins for all time, sat down at the right hand of God"* (Hebrews 10:12, NASB); *"Now where there is forgiveness of these things, there is no longer any offering for sin"* (Hebrews 10:18, NASB 1995). In other words, God paid the price for us, and he wants us to experience what he paid for.

When we pay for something, we don't question whether we should receive delivery of it. If we buy a car or furniture or groceries, we are quite committed to the fact that after paying for them, we get to take them home. Yet when it comes to God receiving what he paid for, we often don't have the same conviction.

But God does. He paid to not only save us from the fires of hell, but the same payment covered our healing, deliverance, prosperity, wellbeing, peace, and everything else you find in his kingdom. And since he paid for it, he has every expectation that we should receive it. He is not holding out on us.

Yet many of us walk around with an orphan spirit that robs us of our identity. That's the thing that tells us we don't belong. It causes us to compare ourselves to others because we think they're better, or more spiritual, or further ahead, or will amount to more than we will. It makes us think that although God may have paid the price in full, we aren't really entitled to it, even if others might be. We know it's been paid for by our heavenly Father, yet we don't contend for it because we're still not convinced we deserve it.

God wants to free us from this way of looking at things. He is for you, and he's willing to go to any length for your benefit. He paid everything to rescue you and rewrite your story.

4. God Has Prepared Incredible Things for You

John 3:16 says, *"For God so loved the world that he gave his only Son, that whoever believes in him should not perish but have eternal life"* (ESV). In Greek, the language the New Testament was written in, this word "life" is *zoe*, which means "the absolute fullness of life." In other words, the God-kind of life, abundant life. And the word "eternal" is *ainios*, which means "perpetual, forever, everlasting." In other words, life "that always has been and always will be." Eternal life is more than how *long* you live; it's also *how* you live. God wants us to learn how to walk with him in a way that we have *abundant life*, not just existing and barely alive.

It's easy to fall into the trap of believing that God has incredible things for us after we die, but that in this life we just need to do our best to get through it. This is simply wrong. God cares about our life now, not just after we die. God has prepared incredible things for us and wants you to dream again. He wants you to let go of the disappointments of the past, to leave the unanswered questions with him, to lay down yesterday's broken dreams, and to stop trying to figure out what went wrong. He wants you to start looking forward rather than behind. Because he has prepared incredible things for you.

5. God Is Constantly Looking for Ways to Include You, Not Exclude You

Contrary to how God may have been portrayed to us, he is never looking for ways to exclude you; he is only looking for ways to include you. John 3:16–17a says, *"For God so loved the world, that he gave his only Son, that whoever believes in him should not perish but have eternal life. For God did not send his Son into the world to condemn the world* …" (ESV, emphasis added).

We tend to approach the kingdom of God like we're trying to figure out the combination to a bike lock after forgetting it. I remember doing this when I was growing up. I had an old bike lock that I hadn't used for a long time and couldn't remember the combination. It had four tumblers that had to line up at the right numbers between zero and nine, in the right order, and then it would unlock. I decided that rather than discarding the lock I would just patiently go through every possible combination. I started at 0000, went to 0001, 0002, and so on until I eventually hit the right combination and the lock opened.

Sometimes it seems like we approach God that way. We act like he's quite mysterious and is waiting for us to hit the right combination before we'll see an answer to our prayers or a breakthrough of some kind. We view God like the person who takes you for your road test when you're trying to get your driver's licence. That's the person with the checklist on the clipboard who sits in the car with you and quietly takes notes as you drive. He doesn't say anything; he just watches you and grades you. And you don't even find out how you did until the end.

It's surprising how often we view our heavenly Father like that. Any infraction and we will be excluded. Any mistake, even if we're unaware of it, and we're rejected. Nothing could be further from the truth. If God wanted to write us off, he wouldn't have to look very hard. But the fact is, God didn't come to condemn. He came to save.

To condemn means to impose a sentence. After being found guilty of a crime, the individual receives their sentence—the price they pay for being guilty. God didn't send Jesus in order to sentence us. He sent Jesus to save us. The question was never whether we were guilty. We were! The question was what God was going to do about that. He chose to dismiss the charges against us after paying our penalty himself.

This doesn't mean that God doesn't distinguish between right and wrong, because he does. It means he doesn't write us off. He doesn't sentence us. He came to save us, and where we fall short, his Holy Spirit is constantly drawing us to that place of forgiveness, freedom, and wholeness. He is constantly looking for ways to include us, not exclude us.

6. God Can Fix What You Have Broken

Our Father wants to fix what we have broken. This is a beautiful revelation. John 3:17 reads, *"For God did not send his Son into the world to condemn the world, but in order that the world might be saved through him"* (ESV, emphasis added).

The world isn't messed up because God messed it up; it's broken because we broke it. And in spite of that, God was willing to be the antidote and wants to fix it. Even now there are things we regret about our lives. None of us are perfect, and some mistakes follow us around as we live out the consequences of them.

It's easy to get stuck here and believe God either can't or doesn't want to use us. But the good news is that God can fix what we have broken. It may not be immediate, and it may not always look like what we want it to look like, but God didn't come to punish us, he came to save us. When we blow it, God always looks for another way to fix it and get us back on course.

The story of the Levites provides a great example of this. Simeon and Levi were two of Jacob's sons who decided to take matters into their own hands when their sister was violated by the prince of the Hivites. In retaliation, they killed every male, including the prince and his dad, the king, captured all the wives and children, and looted all their wealth. When Jacob found out, he was very disturbed.

While Simeon's and Levi's anger and grief were understandable, their response was excessive and disproportionate. They not only sought revenge against the individual who committed the crime but also carried out a violent and brutal massacre against the entire city, including innocent people. Their actions went far beyond seeking justice and escalated the situation to a level of unnecessary violence and bloodshed.

Furthermore, Simeon and Levi had taken matters into their own hands without seeking the guidance or permission of their father, Jacob, who was the head of the family. Jacob had made a covenant with the local inhabitants, promising peaceful relations with them, and Simeon and Levi's violent actions broke that covenant.

All of this troubled Jacob and endangered his entire family. He told Simeon and Levi:

> You have brought trouble on me, by making me odious among the inhabitants of the land, among the Canaanites and the Perizzites; and my men being few in number, they will gather together against me and attack me and I shall be destroyed, I and my household. (Genesis 34:30, NASB 1995)

But Simeon and Levi were unrepentant. Years later, as their father lay on his deathbed, he was blessing each of his sons in turn. When he came to Simeon and Levi, instead of blessing them, he cursed them, saying, "*I will disperse them in Jacob and scatter them in Israel*" (Genesis 49:7b, NASB 1995).

Simeon and Levi had chosen to take things into their own hands, and now they would pay the price for that by being dispersed and scattered in the promised land rather than having land of their own.

However, hundreds of years later, when the descendants of Simeon and Levi formed two of the tribes of Israel, Moses came down from the mountain of the Lord and saw that the people of Israel were worshipping the golden calf that Aaron had made.

> Now when Moses saw that the people were out of control—for Aaron had let them get out of control to the point of being an object of ridicule among their enemies— Moses then stood at the gate of the camp, and said, "Whoever is for the Lord, come to me!" And all the sons of Levi gathered together to him. (Exodus 32:25–26, NASB)

Moses then instructed them to carry out God's judgement because of the people's destructive rebellion and idolatry, saying, "*Every man of you put his sword on his thigh, and go back and forth from gate to gate in the camp, and kill every man his brother, and every man his friend, and every man his neighbor*" (Exodus 32:27b, NASB). In verse 28 we read, "*So the sons of Levi did as Moses instructed, and about three thousand men of the people fell that day*" (NASB). Then Moses said to them, "*Today you have been ordained for the service of the Lord, each one at the cost of his son and of his brother, so that he might bestow a blessing upon you this day*" (Exodus 32:29, ESV).

The day that the Levites turned back to God with all their hearts, God took what they had broken and began to turn it around. The consequences of the curse were turned into a blessing. As priests they wouldn't need land because God himself would be their inheritance. They had brought a curse on themselves, but God turned it into a blessing by giving them the coveted role in the nation of being the priests and stewards of the presence of God. They wouldn't need to farm and toil; they would be completely taken care of. In what seemed like an impossible situation, God intervened and turned it around. As you say "yes" to God, he will do the same for you.

Understanding the heart of our heavenly Father is a lifelong journey. We never "arrive" but are continually growing in our revelation of his love for us and commitment to us. The important thing is that we embark on that journey and allow him to speak words of truth to us both through scripture and in those times when we are quiet before him. As we do, the depths of his love for us will begin to become a reality—not just in our head but in our heart. And this will change everything.

We will stop condemning ourselves because he doesn't condemn us. We'll start forgiving ourselves because he forgives us. We'll stop anticipating judgement and start accepting that he is for us, he is willing to go to any length for our benefit, he is re-writing our story, he is always looking to include us, and he is fixing what we have broken. We'll stop measuring ourselves by ourselves and begin recognizing that our worth is determined by the value he places on us, not our performance.

There is nothing more important than this. It will free us from our own expectations and the expectations of others. It will free us to see that God has incredible plans and a strategy for change to get us there—not just for us, but for others and for our nation. And it will free us to realize that he wants us to be a part of that.

UNDERSTANDING OUR OPPORTUNITY: THE LORD'S PRAYER

When we begin to understand the heart of our Father, it becomes easier to understand the opportunity he has given us. It starts to make sense that when it comes to experiencing and participating in the kingdom of God, we're not waiting for the kingdom to come, but the kingdom is often waiting for us.

At first glance, that might sound a little odd. After all, Jesus taught us to pray "*Thy kingdom come*" (Matthew 6:10a, KJV), so doesn't that mean we're asking and waiting for the kingdom of God to arrive? The short answer is "No." We've seen in previous chapters that the kingdom of God is already here. So if the kingdom of God is here, why would Jesus instruct his disciples to pray that it would come?

The key to understanding the Lord's Prayer is to realize that it doesn't contain any requests. This usually comes as a bit of a shocker because it's the opposite of how we're used to looking at the Lord's Prayer. But it's true. Whether you look at the passage in Matthew 6:9–13 or the one in Luke 11:2–4, the passages don't contain a single request—just commands. Surprisingly, the Lord's Prayer is written in the imperative.

When we use the imperative in English, we are ordering someone to do something. For example, when a parent says to their child, "Come here!" they're not making a request or giving a suggestion. It is a command; they are speaking in the imperative. For this reason, it can be a bit disconcerting to find out that Jesus taught his disciples to pray in the imperative. Was Jesus instructing his disciples to give God orders? No, something else is happening in this passage. Let's take a look.

The first three statements of the Lord's prayer are: hallowed be your name, your kingdom come, and your will be done. All of these are in the third-person imperative. This means that although they're commands, they're not directed toward God (that would be second-person imperative), and neither are they requests. They are commands that are not directed to a specific person.

This can be challenging to understand not only because our high school grammar classes may have been a long time ago, but especially because there is no third-person imperative in the English language. We have a first person imperative ("Let's go!") and a second-person imperative ("Go!"), but no third-person imperative. So if you're not saying "Let's go!" or "You go!" what are you saying?

One scholar explains it this way: "There does not seem to be any sense of the speaker requesting that God allow ("let") these things to occur, or that God make them occur; it is understood that they are to occur."[9] In other words, it's not a request but a command or decree, much like someone in authority might make. They expect their command to be acted on, but it's not directed to a specific person.

We find the same kind of language in the Old Testament when God says in Genesis 1:3, "*Let there be light*" (KJV). This command is also in the third-person imperative, so a better translation would be "Light, exist!" or "Light, be!" It was a command by God himself, yet nobody specifically was being commanded to do this action. Instead, it was a declaration issued by God that carried his creative power.

The Lord's Prayer is an invitation for us to step into our role as co-workers with God. When we declare in faith what the King himself has already declared, we come into agreement with him and participate in the manifestation or extension of his kingdom. Rather than just doing it all himself, God has chosen to partner with us to see the growth of his kingdom on the earth.

This can be a bit much to process all at once, but there is an element of prayer that is intentional and forceful. This doesn't negate the other forms of prayer, such as petition, intercession, or supplication, where we ask God for things. But neither do prayers that are requests negate those that are commands—those that are in the imperative and declare the will and purposes of God.

It's interesting that the next four statements in the Lord's Prayer are also in the imperative, but this time in the second-person imperative, which means we are speaking directly to God. In this case the things we are instructed to pray are things that God himself provides for us: our daily bread, the forgiveness of our trespasses, not being led into temptation, being delivered from evil. All of these are things God does for us or on our behalf.

These prayers are also commands; they are also in the imperative. Are we ordering God to do something? Does he need to be convinced or coerced? No, not at all. Rather, Jesus taught his disciples to pray from a place of absolute confidence and expectation of receiving.

Consider what comes immediately before the Lord's Prayer, when Jesus gives instructions to the disciples on how to pray:

> And when you pray, do not heap up empty phrases as the Gentiles do, for they think that they will be heard for their many words. Do not be like them, for your Father knows what you need before you ask him." (Matthew 6:7–8, ESV)

Jesus essentially tells the disciples, "Don't get caught up in the lie of thinking that whether or not prayers get answered depends on the volume of prayer. God already knows your needs and is more than willing to answer your prayers. He doesn't need convincing; he needs your partnership as a co-worker."

This can be a lot to digest, but it matters. For too long we have misunderstood our role, thinking that we're waiting for God to do something, when He's often waiting for us. Because of our misunderstanding of the Lord's Prayer, we pray for God's kingdom to come like we're waiting for him to send it. Instead, we should be praying from the understanding that we already live in that kingdom, and that our prayers and declarations and obedience will result in its increase in our lives and the lives of those around us.

The story I shared in the last chapter about praying for my mom's tendonitis is a good example of this. God didn't just sovereignly heal her, although that can happen sometimes. But usually, healing is manifested because someone prays a prayer of faith, which can sound like more of a declaration than a request.

The opportunity to partner with God awaits every follower of Christ. Although we enter the kingdom of God as children, the Father doesn't intend for us to perpetually remain as children. We are to grow in our role and responsibility as his *"fellow workers"* (1 Corinthians 3:9, ESV), where we see ourselves as essential partners in the unfolding of his plans and purposes on the earth.

UNDERSTANDING OUR RESPONSIBILITY—THE PARABLE OF THE SOWER

In God's economy, opportunity and responsibility always go together. You don't get one without the other. Understanding our responsibility helps us grow in the reality of walking in the kingdom of God.

Even though the kingdom of God has been on the earth since Jesus came, we weren't automatically included in it when we were born. Rather, when we gave our life to Christ, we were transferred from the domain of darkness into the kingdom of God (Colossians 1:13). In other words, although the kingdom of God is already present, we're not automatically a part of it. This is true not only of entering the kingdom of God when we're born again but also of our ongoing walk with God. We have a role in realizing the fullness of the kingdom of God in our lives and nation.

The Parable of the Sower sheds some important light on our role. Recorded in three of the four gospels, the account from Matthew goes like this:

> Listen! A farmer went out to plant some seeds. As he scattered them across his field, some seeds fell on a footpath, and the birds came and ate them. Other seeds fell on shallow soil with underlying rock. The seeds sprouted quickly because the soil was shallow. But the plants soon wilted under the hot sun, and since they didn't have deep roots, they died. Other seeds fell among thorns that grew up and choked out the tender plants. Still other seeds fell on fertile soil, and they produced a crop that was thirty, sixty, and even a hundred times as much as had been planted! Anyone with ears to hear should listen and understand. (Matthew 13:3–9)

Jesus then explains the meaning of the parable to his disciples privately:

> Now listen to the explanation of the parable about the farmer planting seeds: The seed that fell on the footpath represents those who hear the message about the Kingdom and don't understand it. Then the evil one comes and snatches away the seed that was planted in their hearts. The seed on the rocky soil represents those who hear the message and immediately receive it with joy. But since they don't have deep roots, they don't last long. They fall away as soon as they have problems or are persecuted for

believing God's word. The seed that fell among the thorns represents those who hear God's word, but all too quickly the message is crowded out by the worries of this life and the lure of wealth, so no fruit is produced. The seed that fell on good soil represents those who truly hear and understand God's word and produce a harvest of thirty, sixty, or even a hundred times as much as had been planted! (Matthew 13:18–23)

When this parable is taught in most churches, it is taught as a parable about people getting saved. It illustrates how the same message of salvation can be heard by four different people with four different results. Same word, different results, depending on the condition of the soil. This is an accurate application of the parable, but the full application is much broader. Remember, when Jesus taught this parable, there was no "message of salvation" yet, in the sense that we've come to know it. Jesus had not yet been crucified or resurrected. There was no understanding that he was about to die to atone for the sins of mankind.

While Jesus says that the seed in the parable is the Word of God, he never limits this to a word about salvation. The most detail we get about this "word" is found in Matthew's account, where he refers to it as the *"word of the kingdom"* (Matthew 13:19, ESV). This suggests that the intent of this parable isn't just about receiving salvation but about receiving the kingdom and the things of the kingdom. It's about the Word of God bearing kingdom fruit in our lives. All kinds of fruit. The "Word of God" or the "word of the Kingdom" could be a word of salvation, but it could also be a word of healing, deliverance, prosperity, peace, or any of the things provided through the work of Christ and present in the kingdom of God.

In this parable, Jesus outlines four very different groups of people who find themselves with four different outcomes from the same word. But it can also apply to stages in our life. And from these four stages, we can gain some key insights into what's necessary to walk in the reality of the kingdom.

1. We Must Believe

The first thing this parable shows us is that in order to walk in the reality of the kingdom, we must believe. Everything begins here. It's a fundamental principle of the kingdom taught repeatedly throughout scripture: we must believe in order to receive. It's how we enter the kingdom of God and receive the things of the kingdom once we've entered it. Jesus taught this truth over and over again. In this parable, he said it this way: "*The seed that fell on the footpath represents those who hear the message about the Kingdom and don't understand it. Then the evil one comes and snatches away the seed that was planted in their hearts*" (Matthew 13:19). Hebrews 4:2b sheds some light on why they didn't understand: "*but the word they heard did not profit them, because it was not united by faith in those who heard*" (NASB 1995).

The fact that our faith might make the difference between receiving from God and not receiving from God can make us uncomfortable. It's like too much depends on us. But Jesus was clear on this point: We see repeatedly that those who were able to receive a miracle from Jesus were those who believed. And those who did not believe did not receive (Mark 6:5).

Without faith, we will have difficulty seeing that God can shift our nation. We'll struggle to see the opportunities God is providing to participate in that shift. We'll do our best to live a good life and be a blessing to others, but that's probably as far as we'll be able to see. To shift the nation, we must believe that God wants to do the things he says he wants to do.

This isn't to suggest that just because we believe, the rest will be automatic. If that were the case, the parable would have ended here, and there wouldn't be four different groups of people in this parable. To receive, we must believe, but that's just where we begin our journey.

2. We Must Persevere and Endure

In the second group of people are those who hear the Word, understand it, and receive it with great joy. They believe, but then when difficulty comes, things begin to fall apart. Instead of persevering and enduring in the midst of challenges, they let go of the promise.

> The seed on the rocky soil represents those who hear the message and immediately receive it with joy. But since they don't have deep roots, they don't last long. They fall away as soon as they have problems or are persecuted for believing God's word. (Matthew 13:20–21)

The Word is believed and takes root. But their faith is shallow, so it withers in the face of opposition. With respect to salvation, these people make a commitment and then falter when they face resistance. We see this same principle at work in the lives of those who don't fall away. We can grab hold of the promises of God on a particular issue, but then when opposition comes, we begin to waver and let go.

That opposition might come in the form of circumstances that look contrary to the promise. Or perhaps what we're believing for doesn't arrive as quickly as we expected it to. If we have a shallow root, then when what we believe doesn't match what we see, we'll lose heart. We let go of the Word and stop believing.

All of us are prone to this, which is why perseverance is critical when it comes to apprehending the things of the kingdom and seeing the nation shift. Although we sometimes see noticeable changes in a short period of time, organic and incremental change usually takes place over a longer timeframe and requires steadfast persistence. To walk in the realities of the kingdom, we'll need faith that perseveres and endures, even when the going gets tough and everything looks contrary to what we've been promised.

3. We Must Be Single-Hearted

The third group of people are those who hear the Word, believe the Word, value the Word, and go through opposition in the face of the Word. They never give up and they don't let go. Yet in spite of this, the Word never bears fruit.

How is this possible? The Word is choked by worries, riches, and the desire for other things: *"The seed that fell among the thorns represents those who hear God's word, but all too quickly the message is crowded out by the worries of this life and the lure of wealth, so no fruit is produced"* (Matthew 13:22). Note that in this situation, the person never stops believing. But they still never see the fruit. The Word never brings forth what it could have. Why? They live a distracted life.

When Jesus said the way was narrow, he wasn't joking. Some church culture today likes to tell us that the way is broad: "Do whatever, live however you want, just follow your heart. Don't worry—grace covers it all. God just wants us to enjoy life." This doesn't work in the Christian life. People who live like this aren't able to bear the fruit that God wants them to. If we want to experience more of the fullness of the kingdom, we can't be distracted by the worries of this life, the lure of wealth, and the desire for other things. We are called to live a separated life.

But don't misunderstand—a separated life isn't prescribed by someone's set of rules. It's defined by what we want and how narrow a life we need to live in order to realize it. If you want to be an athlete, you say "no" to a lot of things in order to achieve your goal. There may be nothing wrong with a lot of the things you say "no" to, but you do it anyway because those things are a lower priority and will distract you from your goal.

Some people want faith to see the sick healed and the lame walk, but they don't want faith to live a holy life. They allow bondage to exist in their lives while claiming to be full of faith and wanting to see signs and wonders. In the kingdom of God, we don't have these kinds of options. We are to let the Holy Spirit guide us so that our life reflects the priority we place on him and his kingdom.

A lot of people live ordinary lives and expect extraordinary results. It doesn't work that way. To see a greater manifestation of the kingdom of God on the earth, to the point where our nation begins to shift, will require lives that are sold out to his priorities and separated for his purpose. We must be single-hearted.

4. We Bear the Fruit of the Kingdom

In the fourth group, we see the Word of God bearing much fruit, the power of God beginning to flow, and people's lives being transformed. Sometimes things happen quickly after we lay hold of a promise, but sometimes we have to persevere and press through, undistracted by the voices and temptations around us. It is possible to live a life that is a living example of Mark 4:8: "*Still other seeds fell on fertile soil, and they sprouted, grew, and produced a crop that was thirty, sixty, and even a hundred times as much as had been planted!*"

We were never meant to live the Christian life outside of an atmosphere of experiencing the presence of God, the provision of God, and the power of God. But we have gotten so used to living on a lower level of Christianity that we think living without these things is normal and answered prayer is the exception. This must change.

When we look at the brokenness and dysfunction of society, we can't continue to do what we've always done and expect to get different results. Gone are the days when we can think that having a nice Sunday service and living a nominal Christian life will be enough to impact our nation. We must allow ourselves to be challenged to embrace all that God has made available to us. In order for the nation to shift, we must be able to provide a remedy to those who seek it. Jesus said:

> The Spirit of the Lord is upon me, for he has anointed
> me to bring Good News to the poor. He has sent me
> to proclaim that captives will be released, that the

blind will see, that the oppressed will be set free, and that the time of the Lord 's favor has come. (Luke 4:18–19)

This desperately needs to be the reality of the church today. We live in a time when brokenness runs rampant. We are surrounded by those "... *who call evil good and good evil, who put darkness for light and light for darkness, who put bitter for sweet and sweet for bitter!*" (Isaiah 5:20, ESV). Our nation needs to know that the Spirit of the Lord is present to bring healing and freedom and transformation to those who hunger for it. It needs to know that just as the Holy Spirit empowered Jesus to bring the Good News of the kingdom, the Spirit of God is here to do the same through his people.

We must have a response that addresses the brokenness of our world and doesn't simply try to compel people to comply with Christian standards and lifestyles when they have no power to do so. The bottom line is that we must not only preach the good news of the kingdom, but we must live it and demonstrate it.

Shifting the nation isn't about waiting for the rise of the next political or spiritual superstar. It's about ordinary people getting hold of an extraordinary God, seeing themselves as he sees them, and leaving a mark wherever they go that says, "A little bit of heaven has been here." But walking in the reality of the kingdom is neither automatic nor guaranteed. To be fruitful and effective, we need to understand the opportunity granted to us, the responsibility entrusted to us, and our Father's heart for us. We must realize that the only way to achieve a heavenly vision is to partner with heaven itself.

PART THREE

A Roadmap for Change

UNDERSTANDING THE CONCEPT of organic and incremental change is critical. Constructive change happens slowly over time as people's beliefs and values change. But although the concept is quite simple, the application of this truth in today's world is less clear. How do we get to where we want to go, practically? What is the roadmap for moving forward? I would suggest that the journey has six critical checkpoints along the way:

1. Return: As Christians, we must return to our foundations. We must return to our first love, live life like the claims of Christ are true, and love God with all our heart, soul, mind, and strength. This is not optional; it is imperative. You could call it revival, where that which was once alive but died comes alive again!

2. Restore: As a revived people, we must strengthen and restore our fundamental institutions. Marriages, families, and relationships must be made strong and whole again. Our walk must align with our faith so that our testimony and witness are strong.

3. Reform: We must reform our community, culture, and society by being salt, light, and leaven. We must not retreat but rather engage society around us by being present, by being servants and leaders, and by participating in the conversations and debates taking place. We need to preach the gospel, live the gospel, and impact community values and beliefs with the truth and with our lives.

4. Renew: We must impact and renew our societal infrastructure: our laws, policies, guidelines, expectations, and freedoms. We need to get involved in the decision-making bodies of society at every level with a vision to see health and wholeness come to every part of society.

5. Run: We need to run for public office and be present in the gates of the nation. We must be active in the public square both as office holders and as participants. Our goal is not to have a Christian nation but a healthy country where there is freedom and justice for all.

6. Repeat: The work must not die with us. This is a multi-generational vision. We must actively teach and train the next generation and the one after that on how to hold what has been gained and keep the land that is taken in order to expand the kingdom. Train the people, the thinkers, the leaders of tomorrow rather than entrusting them to the state.

These are critical components on the journey to shifting the nation, which we need to embrace. Understanding and accepting them will ensure that we don't go running after every fad that pops up, thinking there is some secret formula to quick change. There is not. The Church is Christ's agent of change to see more of heaven on earth, and it's up to us to get started.

But how do we practically begin moving down this road? Now that we have a better understanding of God's strategy for change, how do we walk it out? The answer begins by looking at the example of the early church and then considering four spheres of life today: the secret place, the marketplace, the public square, and the place of prayer.

CHAPTER TEN

Learning from the Early Church

IN JUST OVER three hundred years, Christianity went from a small contingent of followers (about 120 followers according to Acts 1:15) to the state religion of the Roman Empire, encompassing over 55 per cent of the population. This kind of exponential growth and influence is almost unbelievable when contrasted to the experience and track record of the church in Canada today.

So how did the early church do it? What can we learn from their experience to help us understand how to effectively promote change in Canada? The book of Acts gives us some insight through its record of the work of the apostles, but the stories contained in Acts only bring us to about 60 AD. What about after the apostles died? What about the three hundred years that followed? What were the key ingredients of the church's continued growth and effectiveness?

Although there are many excellent resources on this issue, one exceptional source of research is Rodney Stark's book, *The Rise of Christianity: How the Obscure, Marginal Jesus Movement Became the Dominant Force in the Western World in a Few Centuries*.[10] By his own admission, Stark is not a Christian, nor is he a historian or New Testament scholar. He's a professor of sociology and comparative religion at the University of Washington. But his preoccupation with the question of how the early church managed such levels of growth and influence led him to examine the issue through the lens of a sociologist and reconstruct the rise of Christianity. His findings are both intriguing and extremely relevant to the church today. And every single one of them points to monumental change that was achieved because it was organic and incremental.

Open Social Networks

Stark begins by outlining the significance of interpersonal relationships in conversion. He notes that cold-calling leads to a conversion once out of a thousand calls, but when the person being contacted is a friend or relative, conversion happens 50 per cent of the time. This is significant because, as Stark points out, a failure to form and sustain attachments to "outsiders" causes movements to lose their ability to grow. He writes: "Successful movements discover techniques for remaining open networks, able to reach out and into new adjacent social networks. And herein lies the capacity of movements to sustain exponential growth rates over a long period of time." [11]

As Stark goes on to explain, "typically people do not seek a faith; they encounter one through their ties to other people who already accept this faith."[12] This means that "religious movements can grow because their members continue to form new relationships with outsiders."[13]

As Christians, we like to think the growth of the early church happened as a result of powerful preaching to large groups, resulting in significant conversions in a short period of time, like when Peter preached in Acts 2 and three thousand people were saved. These kinds of events did happen, and they were important. But as Stark points out, they were the exception, not the rule, and according to simple mathematics, would not have accounted for all the growth experienced by the early church.

Instead, the early Christians emphasized a far more incremental and organic approach. They didn't cut themselves off from those who were non-Christians but maintained their existing social networks and reached out into adjacent ones.

Loving One Another

Stark goes on to note a second reason why the early church flourished. He points out that Judeo-Christian thought brought something new and distinctive into the world: "The linking of a highly social ethical code with religion."[14] He writes:

> The Christian teaching that God loves those who love him was alien to pagan beliefs. Equally alien to paganism was the notion that because God loves humanity, Christians cannot please God unless they love one another. Indeed, as God demonstrates his love through sacrifice, humans must demonstrate their love through sacrifice on behalf of one another. Moreover, such responsibilities were to be extended beyond the bonds of family and tribe, indeed to "all those who in every place call on the name of our Lord Jesus Christ". These were revolutionary ideas.[15]

The church today seems to be looking for something flashier, glitzier, and more show-stopping. We're always looking for the next fad or marketing movement to reach people. How could loving one another be a key to seeing exponential growth in the kingdom? The fact that we're even asking the question shows how far off track we've gotten. The early Christians lived as Christ had taught the disciples, loving God with all their heart, soul, mind, and strength, and loving their neighbours as themselves. They didn't try to overthrow the government or take it over from the inside; they went about the work of the kingdom: sharing the gospel, demonstrating the gospel, and living it out practically, sometimes at great personal expense. And as a result, over the first three centuries they had an unbelievable impact simply by effecting organic, incremental change.

While today's average Christian tends to be somewhat dismissive of organic and incremental growth, Rodney Stark gives practical examples of how living according to the teachings of Christ provided the early Christians with everything they needed to turn the world upside down. They simply lived as Jesus taught them to and found out that Jesus' words were true when he told his disciples:

> A new commandment I give to you, that you love one another: just as I have loved you, you also are to love one another. By this all people will know that you are my disciples, if you have love for one another. (John 13:34–35, ESV)

Laying Down Their Lives

In Chapter 4 of his book, Rodney Stark writes the following:

> In 165, during the reign of Marcus Aurelius, a devastating epidemic swept through the Roman Empire. Some medical historians suspect that it was the first appearance of smallpox in the West. But whatever the actual disease, it was lethal. During the fifteen-year duration of the epidemic, from a quarter to a third of the empire's population died from it, including Marcus Aurelius himself in 180 in Vienna. Then, in 251 a new and equally devastating epidemic again swept the empire, hitting the rural areas as hard as the cities. This time it may have been measles. Both smallpox and measles can produce massive mortality rates when they strike a previously unexposed population.[16]

Stark goes on to outline how these epidemics resulted in a growth surge of Christianity, for somewhat unexpected reasons. First of all,

Christians were better able to cope, which resulted in substantially higher rates of survival. They were able to cope because the teachings of their faith made life meaningful even amid the devastation brought on by the epidemics. They weren't afraid of death, and because of the commandment to love one another, they didn't shy away from helping those who were stricken with illness.

Stark refers to it as "survival rates and the golden rule."[17] He notes the lengthy tribute that the bishop Dionysius wrote, praising the "heroic nursing efforts of local Christians, many of whom lost their lives while caring for others."[18] Dionysius wrote:

> Most of our brother Christians showed unbounded love and loyalty, never sparing themselves and thinking only of one another. Heedless of danger, they took charge of the sick, attending to their every need and ministering to them in Christ, and with them departed this life serenely happy; for they were infected by others with the disease drawing on themselves the sickness of their neighbors and cheerfully accepting their pains. Many, in nursing and curing others, transferred their death to themselves and died in their stead. ... The best of our brothers lost their lives in this manner ...[19]

Dionysius noted that this kind of behaviour was starkly different from that demonstrated by those who were not Christians:

> The heathen behaved in the very opposite way. At the first onset of the disease, they pushed the sufferers away and fled from their dearest, throwing them into the roads before they were dead and treated unburied corpses as dirt, hoping thereby to avert the spread and contagion of the fatal disease; but do what they might, they found it difficult to escape.[20]

Stark notes that the impact of this was three-fold. First of all, the practical benefit of receiving even the most rudimentary nursing care had a significant impact on survival rates of those infected. Medical experts have estimated that nursing care, even without medications, would have cut the mortality rate by two-thirds or more. This means that while the general population was experiencing a mortality rate of about 30 per cent, amongst those who received nursing care from the Christians the rate would have dropped to about 10 per cent.

Secondly, this would have resulted in a much superior Christian survival rate, which would have led to a much larger proportion of Christians who were immune and thus able to be active in nursing without contracting the disease a second time. As Stark writes:

> In this way was created a whole force of miracle workers to heal the "dying". And who was to say that it was the soup they so patiently spooned to the helpless that healed them, rather than the prayers the Christians offered on their behalf.[21]

Although Stark fails to understand the power of prayer, he accurately observes that the practical care provided by Christians increased the survival rate of those who received that care.

Thirdly, Stark notes that the witness of those who were willing to risk their lives for the benefit of others would have left an indelible mark on the survivors. With the devastation left in the wake of the epidemics, non-Christian survivors would have been drawn into the communities of Christians who cared for them in their illness, and also drawn into the faith that was a light in a time of terrible darkness.

This is so simple yet so profound: One of the reasons the early church grew like it did is because they were willing to lay down their lives for others. Although the application of that may be very different for us today, the need to do so remains the same.

Valuing What God Values

Christ and his apostles taught that Christians were not to treat people differently depending on their sex, nationality, or economic status. Following these teachings had a direct and substantive impact on the growth of the early church. Rodney Stark explains it this way:

> Amidst contemporary denunciations of Christianity as patriarchal and sexist, it is easily forgotten that the early church was so especially attractive to women that in 370 the emperor Valentinian issued a written order to Pope Damasus I requiring that Christian missionaries cease calling at the homes of pagan women. Although some classical writers claim that women were easy prey for any "foreign superstition," most recognized that Christianity was unusually appealing because within the Christian subculture women enjoyed far higher status than did women in the Greco-Roman world at large. [22]

Stark explains that unlike the rest of the Greco-Roman world, the Christian faith valued women equally to men. Unlike the rest of the world around them, Christian doctrines prohibited infanticide, abortion, adultery, and divorce. The practical result of this was that Christianity was very attractive to women. But secondly, by prohibiting infanticide and abortion, Christians removed major causes of the gender imbalance that existed in the Greco-Roman culture, where the number of men had previously vastly outnumbered women.

Consequently, not only was there a much higher birth rate in Christian communities than in the society around them, but non-Christian men were drawn into Christianity because of the desire to find a wife and the refusal of Christian women to marry non-Christians. Stark identifies both of these as factors in the early growth of Christianity and goes into great detail to demonstrate the significant impact these would have had on the numerical growth of Christians.

Stark's entire book is riveting and contains many more examples of factors that led to the exponential growth of Christianity in the first three centuries. And although the world we live in today is much different than that of two thousand years ago, these factors illustrate a simple truth that remains just as relevant today: The early Christians impacted their world in unbelievably significant ways because they not only shared the gospel but lived it out in real life. Theirs was not a Sunday-only gospel. They didn't cordon themselves off from the world but lived their Christianity openly and selflessly and often at significant personal cost. As they did so, they slowly but surely changed their world.

The early church wasn't focused on radical and directed change. There is no avoiding this truth. They were deeply invested in the organic and incremental change that comes by living as Christ commanded and demonstrating the reality of the love of God and the kingdom of God in both word and deed.

Today, the Christian church seems to be constantly looking for the next big thing, or the next revelation, or the next move of God, when what we really need has been here all along since the time of Christ. In order to have a lasting impact on society, the roadmap begins by following the example of Jesus, who separated Himself to the Father's will, laid down his life in service for others, and walked in the authority given to him by the Father. Once again, we must realize that the only way to achieve a heavenly vision is to partner with heaven itself.

CHAPTER ELEVEN

Christians in the Secret Place

SHIFTING THE NATION begins in the "secret place"—the place where we draw away from everything else and draw near to God. It's the place where we meet with him in private for prayer, worship, Bible reading, and just listening to him. It's here that the overwhelming task of shifting the nation is placed into its proper perspective and kept in its rightful place, where everything comes to a place of peace as we lay it at the feet of our heavenly Father.

One thing that differentiates Christianity from other religions is that we're called to place our dependence solely on God. God continually told his people not to have any other gods or idols in their lives. He was to be the one and only. But since we don't usually have little wooden or porcelain gods in our homes, we struggle to understand what a "god" might be in our life. The English language doesn't help us much here, because we tend to say things like, "He idolizes that person," which makes us think that placing great value on something could make it an idol in our life. But that's not necessarily so. The best explanation of a god or an idol in the twenty-first century is a very simple one: our gods or idols are those things in which we place our hope, expectation, and dependency.

God wants us totally dependent on him. We may have a job that provides a stream of income, but behind that job is God our Father, who provides for us through that job. God told the Israelites to never forget that it was he who gave them the power to create wealth.

When we start looking to our own strength and power as the source of good things in our life, we're off track, and our effectiveness in extending the kingdom of God will be limited. But when we recognize that he is our provider, healer, deliverer, and source, and that his Word illuminates our path and his hand directs us in the way we should go, then he can work through us.

This is critical when considering the need to shift our nation. Such an assignment is nothing less than overwhelming, and as soon as we start leaning on our own strength, we begin to become cynical, suspicious of others, judgemental, and negative. Criticisms begin to pour out of our mouths. Even though what we're saying might be true, that doesn't make it right.

This was the position the nation of Israel found itself in when it sent out the twelve spies to spy out the promised land. All twelve saw exactly the same thing. But when they came back to report to Moses and the Israelites, ten of them were negative, pessimistic, and full of unbelief. Only two, Joshua and Caleb, gave a good report.

The difference between these two groups was this: Joshua and Caleb were placing their confidence and expectation in God, whereas the others were placing it in themselves. Just look at what the ten had to say: *We are not able to go up against the people, for they are stronger than we are*" (Numbers 13:31, ESV). The naysayers were looking at the challenge in light of their own strength and ability.

Joshua and Caleb, on the other hand, said this:

> If the Lord is pleased with us, then he will bring us into the land and give it to us … Only do not rebel against the Lord; and do not fear the people of the land, for they shall be our prey. Their protection has

been removed from them, and the Lord is with us;
do not fear them. (Numbers 14:8–9, NASB)

Their confidence was in God and in God alone.

Many Christians today are desperate to see the nation of Canada shift, but their confidence is not in God. As a result, they sometimes do more harm than good. They mean well, and they might even see the problem accurately, but they don't understand the solution. They are determined to fight to regain what they feel they have lost, but they lack the godly wisdom, strategy, and the anointing necessary to do so. Sarai knew that God had promised a son to Abraham but saw no fulfilment of the promise, so she took matters into her own hands and had Abraham sleep with her maidservant, Hagar. This attempt to solve their problem in the "flesh" rather than in the "spirit" yielded untold grief, not joy and victory. The same can be true of us.

If we're going to see our nation shift, it's not going to happen because of our strength, wisdom, strategies, or determination. Yes, it will require dedication, hard work, and a focused life, but it will only come to pass as we partner with the God of heaven to bring a bit of heaven to earth. This is the significance of the secret place. It's where we meet with God personally. It's where he speaks to us, ministers to us, and teaches us. It's the place of preparation, equipping, and anointing.

It is worth remembering that even Jesus spent time with the Father before he began his earthly ministry. From as early as twelve years old we see that his time with the Father had already produced a wealth of wisdom and insight as he spoke with the leaders in the temple. And once his earthly ministry began, he regularly stole away to be alone with God, sometimes spending all night in prayer. Although he was the Son of God, Jesus acknowledged that, *"Truly, truly, I say to you, the Son can do nothing of his own accord, but only what he sees the Father doing. For whatever the Father does, that the Son does likewise"* (John 5:19, ESV).

This is our pattern, and it's a pattern found only in the secret place. Not conferences, not books, not sermons, but in time spent alone with the Father, coming to understand who he is, how he sees us, and what he has given us to do.

As Christians, we simply can't afford to live without it. If Jesus needed it, we need it all the more. It's the place where we are to live and minister out of, where we are changed and equipped to bring change to the lives of those around us. It serves as the foundation and the launching pad for everything else we do in our life.

And without it, we will not shift the nation.

CHAPTER TWELVE

Christians in the Marketplace

AS CHRISTIANS, EVERYTHING we do is to be done as service to God. That's why Paul exhorted the church at Colossae by writing, *"Whatever you do, work heartily, as for the Lord and not for men"* (Colossians 3:23, ESV). We tend to divide our lives into compartments of the sacred and the secular, but in reality there is no such separation. Our entire life and everything we do is sacred and is to bring glory to God. Understanding this is critical. Our time in the secret place is essential and foundational, but it's no more holy or spiritual than our time in the marketplace.

It took me years to understand this truth. When I first started my walk with Christ, I knew that he was calling me into full-time ministry. And in my understanding, that could only mean one thing: I was to be a pastor. So for the next few years I went to Bible college, until I was asked to join the team of pastors at a local church in Regina. For the next seven years I served in this capacity and loved it. I knew I was doing what God had called me to do, even when it was difficult.

But as time went along, I began to feel that God was beginning to lead me in a different direction, from full-time ministry in the church to ministry in the marketplace. He eventually used circumstances to force this transition, and when it happened, I felt both excited and lost. What was I going to do now?

I had no training other than Bible school, and my experience of doing summer ranch work through high school and college was not going to help me much in the city. I decided the best thing to do would be to lean on my administrative abilities and look for employment in that field.

In those days, the primary place to find job postings was in the "classifieds" section of the newspaper. I scanned those ads for six months and submitted an untold number of applications. But one day I came across an advertisement for an office manager with an organization called the Association of Saskatchewan Taxpayers. I had no idea what the Association of Saskatchewan Taxpayers (AST) was, but I applied for the job and was given the position.

I anticipated that my life was now going to be neatly divided into two spheres: my ministry with my wife leading worship at church, and my employment as an office manager earning a living. But God had a very different perspective. He began to show me that the Spirit of the Lord was upon me not just to do things in the church but also in the marketplace. I learned about Bezalel in the book of Exodus, who was a skilled craftsman commissioned by God to oversee the construction of the tabernacle.

> Then the Lord said to Moses, "Look, I have specifically chosen Bezalel son of Uri, grandson of Hur, of the tribe of Judah. I have filled him with the Spirit of God, giving him great wisdom, ability, and expertise in all kinds of crafts. He is a master craftsman, expert in working with gold, silver, and bronze. He is skilled in engraving and mounting gemstones and in carving wood. He is a master at every craft!" (Exodus 31:1–5)

It was a revelation to me that God would fill people with the Spirit of God to give *"great wisdom, ability, and expertise in all kinds of crafts."* Yet there it was, right in the Bible.

I began to see this truth in other passages, such as the story of Joseph:

> The Lord was with Joseph, and he became a successful man, and he was in the house of his Egyptian master. His master saw that the Lord was with him and that the Lord caused all that he did to succeed in his hands. (Genesis 39:2–3, ESV)

When Joseph was thrown in jail, this favour followed him:

> But the Lord was with Joseph in the prison and showed him his faithful love. And the Lord made Joseph a favorite with the prison warden. Before long, the warden put Joseph in charge of all the other prisoners and over everything that happened in the prison. The warden had no more worries, because Joseph took care of everything. The Lord was with him and caused everything he did to succeed. (Genesis 39:21–23)

As the story goes on, we see God using Joseph to save an entire generation by giving him favour and wisdom and strategy. It didn't matter what he was given to do, God was there to enable Joseph to do far beyond what his own abilities would have allowed him to accomplish.

This is the revelation we need to get deep into our hearts: God considers everything we do to be sacred unto him, whether it's in the secret place or the marketplace. And he wants to anoint us for those things, which will enable us to be better at them than we are on our own. God doesn't want us to struggle in our own strength to do what he has given us to do. He wants to empower us to do it under his grace, his anointing, and his direction.

When I began to grasp this truth, I began purposefully turning my attention and my expectation toward God to help me do a good job. And as I did, I excelled. It wasn't long until I was promoted from office manager to research associate. Then from research associate to provincial coordinator and finally senior operations officer. I had taken a job in a field I knew little about, but as I leaned into the Father for wisdom, anointing, and understanding, he empowered me to excel. This doesn't mean that I didn't work hard and study hard—I did, just like Joseph probably had to. But I began to perform better than I was able to in my own strength.

The purpose of the AST was to promote the responsible and efficient use of tax dollars. So we would keep a close eye on government spending with a view to encouraging efficiency and accountability. We'd watch for anything that ran contrary to these principles and bring it to the attention of the public, knowing that the best way to banish darkness is simply to shine a light on it.

In the course of this work, we would often find God giving us wisdom and strategy, and leading us to see things others had missed. For example, we discovered that when Saskatchewan Members of the Legislative Assembly (MLAs) were defeated in an election, they were permitted to keep all of their constituency office furnishings and equipment, even though these had been purchased with tax dollars. That meant any computers, printers, fax machines (those were still a thing then), desks, cabinets—everything—would get loaded into a truck and became the personal property of the defeated MLA. We called it the "Clean Office Policy"—everything got cleaned out.

This policy had been in place for a long time, and nobody had noticed it. But in the course of examination, God brought it to our attention, and we simply made it public and denounced it as an inappropriate use of tax dollars. As you can imagine, the public pressure almost immediately resulted in the cancelation of this policy. It couldn't stand under the light, and it crumbled.

In the larger scheme of the province's annual budget, this wasn't a big thing. But in terms of honesty, transparency, and public accountability, it was huge. The exposure and subsequent cancellation of the policy reverberated across the country as other provinces were then exposed to the same examination of their policies.

In the coming years and decades, this pattern repeated itself over and over and over. As I intentionally leaned into God for wisdom, understanding, strategy, and the words to express it all, I constantly found myself empowered to do better than I was able to in my own strength.

Later, I ran my own web design business for a few years. I had done some web design in the past for the organizations I'd worked for and a few jobs on the side, and I was fairly good at it. But now I was launching out with no clientele, no job leads, and no public profile. It was a ground-level start-up.

The first few months were gruelling. I did everything that needed to be done, including advertising, cold-calling businesses, and working my contacts. I got some work but, as is normal in the beginning stages, work was slow.

This all changed virtually overnight.

In the middle of a national election campaign, I received a call from a key person in Steven Harper's campaign. He said that Harper was being accused of plagiarizing me, as the media had found similarities between a speech he had given and columns I had previously written on the same subject. The similarities were real, but the accusation of plagiarizing was nonsense. I had actually written that speech for Steven Harper, which was the reason for the similarities with my other writings.

The campaign team needed a statement from me explaining this back story. I was happy to provide one and suggested that I post it on my web design business website. They agreed. When I did so, news organizations such as CTV, CBC, and *Macleans* magazine all linked to the statement on my website. And as anyone with an understanding of Search Engine Optimization would understand, this gave an immediate bounce to my ranking in search engine results.

I won't bore you with the details, but suffice it to say that, at the time, Google saw links to your website as votes of confidence. Links from low-ranked sites didn't amount to much, but those from highly ranked sites counted for a lot. My ranking shot up from around forty-something in the search results to number two. And it stayed there for years.

Choosing to place the statement on my website was no accident. As I was speaking to the campaign worker about the situation, the idea dropped into my head in a way that I knew it was a "God thought." It was a small window of opportunity for which God gave me a simple strategy that had significant implications for my business.

I could tell many stories that illustrate this truth: God wants to anoint you for what you do in the marketplace, and as he does, you will experience his favour and blessing! God's anointing is not just for preachers or pastors or worship leaders but for all of us in every corner of the marketplace.

God wants to strategically position you for this season. He wants to enable you to do more than you can in your own strength. And if we're going to see the nation shift, it's imperative that we get a hold of this truth. If our wisdom, effort, and strategies were enough to shift the nation, it would have shifted long ago. But they are not. We must learn to "lean into God" and allow him to work through us to bring a little bit of heaven into the places where we live and walk and work every day.

For each of us, this looks different, depending on where God has placed us. But the strategy of heaven is to use us in every situation to transform it in small and large ways. Christians in every walk of life and level of leadership should learn to tap into the resources of heaven to bring excellence to their work and blessing to their employers and customers.

As Christians, we have a "God advantage" because he partners with us. We need to begin to expect this, anticipate it, ask for it, and watch for it. We should expect to do things better than we are able. We should expect that God will give us the answers to many of the challenges facing society and business today. We should expect to have creative ideas and breakthrough inventions and problem-solving solutions. We should expect to change the atmosphere in our jobs, schools, and neighbourhoods. We should contend for the wisdom, strategy, and insights of heaven to cascade through us into the world around us, making it a better place for everyone.

Shifting the nation doesn't happen like an earthquake. It's more like a slow flooding process. And partnering with God in the marketplace is key to this. As Christians, we operate with an advantage because we are in partnership with the most-high God.

CHAPTER THIRTEEN

Christians in the Public Square

IN 2003, MY wife and I moved to Edmonton to work with an emerging organization called the Citizen's Centre for Freedom and Democracy (CCFD). The name was almost as cumbersome as the organization's mandate, which was effectively to see a renewal and rebalancing of the federation of Canada. This sounds like a mouthful, but it essentially comes down to this: Canada was designed to be a federation of provinces and functions best when it acts like a federation.

Most people are surprised to learn that the federal government was created by the provinces—not the other way around. Provinces are sovereign in their own right and not simply subdivisions of the nation. This means they have significant powers, and the Constitution provides a clear delineation between what is federal jurisdiction and what is provincial jurisdiction. The problem is that, over time, the reach of the federal government has gradually increased, along with its influence over provincial matters and spending priorities.

Healthy federalism is necessary to ensure a decentralization of the decision-making power in the country. This provides a check on the power and control of the federal government, while giving an appropriate level of autonomy to the provinces. The more centralized the nation becomes, the less restraint there is on the federal government, and the more it tries to shape the country according to its own vision. This vision is almost always reflective of the values and priorities of elites and powerbrokers rather than the average person. And historically, the inevitable outcome of this has almost never been good.

We saw a critical need to advance the idea of healthy federalism and encourage the provinces to retake their rightful and constitutional place in the nation's decision-making process. The best place to do this, we felt, was the province of Alberta. Alberta was the least dependent on federal transfers, had a history of standing up to the federal government, and embodied the boldness and courage a region would need to press for a realignment in federal/provincial relations. Thus, the Citizens Centre for Freedom and Democracy was born.

For a number of years, the CCFD pursued the tried-and-true course of promoting change by informing and empowering the people. But after the retirement of Ralph Klein as premier of the province, it became apparent that while the people of Alberta were supportive of Alberta taking a greater leadership role within the federation, the government of Alberta was not. After decades in power, the Progressive Conservative Party of Alberta had become a dynasty and was no longer dynamically representing or responding to the people of the province. The only solution was to change the party in power with one that would advance the province's rightful place in the federation.

The decision was made to use the organization's membership to help launch a new provincial party—the Wildrose Party of Alberta—wind the CCFD down, and focus on the political implementation of the solution. It was a paradigm shift for us, and one that cost us everything we had built. But we knew it was the right decision.

The journey that followed had its ups and downs. As described in Chapter Two, change always takes longer than you think it will, costs more than you expect it will, and the outcome is never as perfect as you envisioned it would be. Such was the reality that unfolded.

The Wildrose Party merged with the Alliance Party and became known as the Wildrose Alliance. Link Byfield, our colleague at the CCFD, recruited Danielle Smith to run for the leadership of the party, and after she won, the Wildrose Alliance went on to become the official opposition.

Then things got stormy. In an attempt to bring conservatives back together, Danielle, along with a number of other Wildrose MLAs, decided to cross the floor to join the Progressive Conservative party. The province was not impressed. In the next general election, the Progressive Conservatives were booted from power and a New Democratic Party government was elected for the first time in Alberta. It would take another four years before the Wildrose and the Progressive Conservatives would unite under a new party called the United Conservative Party (UCP) and form government under the leadership of Jason Kenney.

For a while it looked like Premier Kenney would be the one to promote true federalism by standing up to the federal government's constant overreach. But COVID interrupted everything, and UCP members who were unhappy with Kenney's handling of the pandemic initiated a leadership review, which resulted in Jason Kenney's resignation.

Today, as this is being written, Danielle Smith is once again leader of the party and premier of the province. She is taking determined steps to push the federal government out of provincial jurisdiction and bring about true federalism in Alberta. As imperfect as some of her efforts may have been, this shift is badly needed in Canada.

There is, however, no guarantee on how things will go, because a million things could go wrong. But this is the point: change that begins on the ground and in the hearts of men and women must eventually find its expression in the institutions of power, including the halls of legislatures and Parliament. And this means that Christians must be present in the public square.

KNOWING OUR MISSION IN THE PUBLIC SQUARE

But just being present in the public square isn't enough. We must know what we are to do when we get there and how we're to do it. In a nutshell, we need wisdom.

In general, the objectives of Christians who are active in the public square seem to fall somewhere between striking back and taking over. Striking back is a defensive posture. This is the cohort of Christians who believe that Christianity is under attack by the state. As described in earlier chapters, they believe that policies and laws that don't conform to the Christian faith are an outright assault on the church, which warrants a counterattack. The objective was initially to protect the state preference enjoyed by the church, and after losing that battle it transitioned into fighting to not lose more ground.

Taking over is an offensive position. This is the cohort of Christians who believe, for a wide range of reasons, that Christian values should be imposed on others using the power of the state. Legislation and legislators are viewed through a polarized lens and cast as either good or evil and need to be supported or opposed. The objective is to win legislative and policy battles by overpowering the opposing voices and hopefully transforming Canada into a Christian state—if not overtly, then at least in practice.

At their core, both of these objectives are fundamentally wrong and ineffective. In fact, a more accurate adjective to describe them would be "harmful." The idea that Christians must compel society to conform to our standards and moral obligations is contrary to the heart of the gospel. And if we bring this attitude into the public square, we do more harm than good.

God is deeply invested in freedom of choice. His primary strategy for change is that which happens from the bottom up and from the heart out. While he could impose righteousness on a nation in a heartbeat, he does not. He's after the hearts of men and women. And whereas our engagement in the public square should reflect this priority, neither of the two approaches above do that.

So what is our objective in the public square? I would propose that, fundamentally, it consists of two things: to protect freedom of belief for everyone so that the gospel can be lived and shared without hindrance.

This is the message of 1 Timothy 2:1–2:

> First of all, then, I urge that supplications, prayers, intercessions, and thanksgivings be made for all people, for kings and all who are in high positions, that we may lead a peaceful and quiet life, godly and dignified in every way. (ESV)

The objective isn't to use the power of the state to impose our beliefs on others but to preserve the freedoms of all citizens so that we are free to live out the command of Jesus:

> Go therefore and make disciples of all nations, baptizing them in the name of the Father and of the Son and of the Holy Spirit, teaching them to observe all that I have commanded you. (Matthew 28:19–20a, ESV)

Nowhere does Jesus suggest that the power of the state should be used as a tool to further the kingdom of heaven. (If we understood the implications of trying to do so, it would terrify us.) Instead, the state and its ministers are repeatedly depicted by scripture as having a God-given role in protecting freedoms and ensuring justice so that its citizens can live peacefully and prosper.

The challenge is that there is no clear playbook on how Christians should walk this out. And there are strong convictions on all sides that propel Christians into the positions and strategies they take on the issues.

Consider, for example, the issue of gay marriage. On July 20, 2005, Canada became the fourth country in the world to legalize same-sex marriage. It had already been legalized in eight out of ten provinces (we tend to forget this) but received federal approval with the passing of the *Civil Marriage Act*. This move to legalize same-sex marriage was contested vehemently by many faith-based groups, including Christians. The core of the opposition was based on a conviction that it was contrary to God's pattern and harmful to the foundational role that families play in society.

Proponents of same-sex marriage didn't see it this way at all. For them it was a question of equal rights: Why should they not have the right to marry the person they love just like heterosexual couples? The Supreme Court of Canada had already ruled back in 1995 in *Egan v. Canada* that sexual orientation was a prohibited basis of discrimination under the Charter of Rights. So as far as the gay community was concerned, this change was long overdue.

The challenge for Christians after living with state preferential treatment for so long is envisioning and adjusting to life without it. The Christian argument against gay marriage is correct for Christians, but it carries little weight with non-Christians. Suggesting that it should then becomes the basis for the assertion that it's appropriate and necessary to use the power of the state to impose biblical standards on all of society. I would argue that such a top-down approach to transforming a nation is fundamentally and dangerously wrong.

This statement will elicit a range of reactions, which demonstrates the challenge of writing about how the body of Christ can effectively promote change in Canada. Without using specific examples, the whole exercise is a bit theoretical. But by using specific examples, you risk losing the ear of all those people who take a different position on that particular issue. And although this book seeks to communicate the primary principle of bottom-up change, there are implications of this understanding that must be wrestled with. My hope is that readers with a different view on this issue will push through and hear me out. Having considered what I have to say, each is obviously free to make up their own mind in the end.

Regrettably, however, this is one of the greatest weaknesses of Christians when it comes to relating to the world around us: Too many take no interest in actually trying to understand people whose positions are different from their own. Instead, they associate only with people who agree with them, and thus become socially ghettoized in their outlook and impact.

While there's no obligation to agree with the views of others when they conflict with our understanding of scripture, there is a strategic obligation to at least understand their position so that we can communicate respectfully, interact meaningfully, and respond intelligently to their objections. Furthermore, in addition to our strategic obligation, we have a biblical mandate to acknowledge the image of God in every person and walk with them in love, even if we don't agree with them. How we treat people matters—not because of what we might get out of it but because of whom we represent.

Our objective as Christians is not to conform the laws of the nation to mirror our beliefs but to ensure that the laws of the nation permit us the freedom to reach the hearts of those around us who don't yet know the love of Christ. This doesn't mean that it's wrong to carry Christian views into the public square. But it does mean that our goal should never be to impose them on those who don't share them. This is a critical distinction that we must not miss.

As the Church of Christ, the most powerful weapon we have is the power of the gospel to change the hearts and minds of fellow Canadians. The power of the law may transform people's behaviour, but it won't transform their hearts. If we have confidence in the power of the gospel, then we must protect the freedom of others to either follow Christ or not follow him. Why does this matter? Because if we try to shift a nation without changing the hearts of people, we may see some temporary change, but it won't be sustainable, and it won't be the transformative change that is possible because of the gospel.

Canada is not a Christian nation, and it's time that Christians accept that reality. For many, this will be a difficult paradigm shift. There has long been talk in Christian circles about how Canada was formed on a Christian foundation, and that this presents an obligation and even a right to continue in that fashion. In reality, however, there is no such obligation or right. We must influence society by being servants and representatives of the kingdom of heaven, just as the early church had to do while living under Roman rule. We are welcomed to be part of the process that determines public policy and the laws that govern our nation, but we don't get to unilaterally dictate the outcome.

OUR INVITATION INTO THE PUBLIC SQUARE

After the last few decades of seeing policies move in a direction that conflicts with traditional values, many Christians have developed a "bunker" mentality in which they believe we are under siege and not welcome in the public square. It comes as a surprise to them to learn that this is not the case.

This isn't to suggest that the entire nation is encouraging Christians to bring their faith into the public square and openly express their values and viewpoints. There are, and will always be, those who prefer to push out or shout down any voices that are contrary to their own positions or worldview. But this does not remove our rightful and legitimate place in the public square.

There are many good books on the subject of religious freedom in Canada, and the topic is worth delving into deeply. But we won't do so here. Instead, I want to simply make one point. Rather than being pushed out of the public square, Christians and the church have been invited into it. The popular myths that suggest otherwise are simply wrong. Let's take a look at them.

MYTH: Religion Is to Be a Private Affair and Has No Place in the Public Square

The privatization of religion is essentially the push to see the public square sanitized of all things religious. It espouses the idea that any reference to, or representation of, religion has no place in the public square and should be confined to the private realm. While many religion-haters like to promote this position as the necessary outcome, it has been flatly rejected by the Supreme Court of Canada.

In April 2015, the Supreme Court of Canada (SCC) ruled in *Mouvement laïque québécois v. Saguenay (Saguenay)*[23] that the City of Saguenay in Quebec could not begin its municipal council meetings with prayer. On its surface, the decision appeared to be an endorsement of state-sponsored secularism. It was not. Instead, the judgement clarified that while religious rites and observances can't be imposed on individuals by the state, those individuals continue to possess a Charter right to practise their faith openly in the public square.

In its decision, the Court said:

> By expressing no preference [on religion or belief], the state ensures that it preserves a neutral public space that is free of discrimination and in which true freedom to believe or not to believe is enjoyed by everyone equally, given that everyone is valued equally. I note that a neutral public space does not mean the homogenization of private players in that space. Neutrality is required of institutions and the state, not individuals.[24]

Although the practice may appear different in real life, the Supreme Court of Canada itself has ruled that there is room for belief and non-belief in the public space. It's the state that must be neutral with respect to religious belief, not the citizens.

MYTH: Churches and Religious Groups Have No Place in the Public Square

The Court went even further to explicitly affirm the right of churches and religions to participate in the public space. It said:

> The concept of neutrality allows churches and their members to play an important role in the public

space where societal debates take place, while the state acts as an essentially neutral intermediary in relations between the various denominations and between those denominations and civil society. [25]

Rather than shutting down the voice of religion in Canada's public spaces, the Supreme Court of Canada clearly and unequivocally confirmed that the voice of the church and its members is important and constitutionally protected. Any suggestion to the contrary is simply wrong.

MYTH: Separation of Church and State Is Required

Christians are frequently lectured on the need for separation of church and state. This argument gets dragged out in various contexts with the undisguised objective of removing religious values and discourse from the public space. Yet in spite of these persistent arguments, the Supreme Court of Canada is on record stating the following:

> True neutrality is concerned not with a strict separation of church and state on questions related to religious thought. The purpose of neutrality is instead to ensure that the state is, and appears to be, open to all points of view regardless of their spiritual basis. Far from requiring separation, true neutrality requires that the state neither favour nor hinder any religion, and that it abstain from taking any position on this subject. [26]

Separation of church and state is not a Canadian concept. Instead, the state is required to be neutral, and the church is free to engage in the public square and make its views and beliefs known. If you've heard the contrary opinion for any length of time, this may come as a pleasant surprise to you. Nothing in law restricts a

Christian's ability to participate in the public square, and that includes the right to express his or her beliefs.

In Canada, we have religious freedom. It's true that this freedom is under attack from some quarters of society, but such opposition doesn't eliminate our rights and freedoms. Rather, this religious freedom protects all religious beliefs (and non-belief), and they are all free to participate in the public square, with none being granted a favoured place by the state.

It comes as a surprise to many Christians to learn that Christian meetings are alive and well on Parliament Hill and meet regularly. Every week that Parliament is sitting, a small group of Christian MPs and Senators from different political parties gather for the Parliamentary Prayer Breakfast. This breakfast is a non-partisan gathering where Christian parliamentarians have the opportunity to eat together, share with one another, and pray for one another. They come to know one another better and have an opportunity to recognize the presence of God in each other.

On Fridays at noon, another group meets for staff members. It's called Parliament Hill Christian Fellowship and has been meeting since 1976. It was started by staffers who worked in the Prime Minister's Office when Pierre Elliot Trudeau was the Prime Minister and has been going ever since. It's a non-partisan, ecumenical, Christ-centred meeting for Christians on and around Parliament Hill and takes place in the chapel in the East Block building. The meetings include fellowship, food, and a short talk to encourage staffers in their faith and professional lives. It's a great opportunity for Christians on Parliament Hill to connect with other Christians.

These meetings are important not just because they minister to Christians on Parliament Hill, but because they're an opportunity to exercise the right to religious freedom that we still enjoy in Canada.

The Supreme Court's decision in the Saguenay case didn't establish those rights, but it did reinforce them. And while the Saguenay decision doesn't answer all of our questions or give clarity to all of the issues, we must acknowledge and affirm what the Court has made clear: the state is to be neutral with respect to religion, and people of faith or no faith are to have equal access to the public square and public office, and they have equal opportunity to influence public policy. If we as Christians fail to apprehend this, then we are forfeiting a great opportunity.

AVOIDING PITFALLS IN THE PUBLIC SQUARE

Being informed and active in the public square brings with it certain dangers. Although these dangers are probably not what you'd expect, they need to be acknowledged and purposefully avoided. If we fail to do so, they will make us ineffective and even disqualify us from having a significant impact.

In order to bear good fruit and be as effective as possible, there are some things we need to be careful to avoid.

Blaming the Government

Contrary to popular belief, when you see a problem in society, it likely wasn't caused by the government. Instead, government is almost always a reflection of the pre-existing reality of the problem, not the root of it. Similarly, if something is missing in society, the solution is rarely more government. In fact, if history is any teacher, we should have learned long ago that more government, more laws, and more policies usually make things worse, not better.

Yet for some reason we find it easy to blame the government for the conditions around us and then insist that the government fix those problems. This is ironically contradictory but nonetheless a popular viewpoint.

The predisposition to blame the government is prevalent in society in general, but for some reason it seems to be even more common amongst Christians. Perhaps it's because we believe the change in values and norms over the years has resulted from changing laws and policies. Perhaps it's because we carry a deep respect for the power of government due to our inherent belief that good government (God's government) will one day rectify all the problems in the world. Perhaps it's just because it's easier to blame the government than to look more deeply (and honestly) at what's going on.

There's no question that governments have significant and sustained impacts on society. Bad government can ruin a society, and good government can restore it. But the roots of that change are rarely found within the government itself; they are found within society. This is why it's imperative that we stop blaming government. Blaming government distracts us from the real problem and focuses our attention and expectation on things that will never deliver the result we're looking for. It blinds us to the real solutions that are achieved through organic and incremental change and shifts our attention toward radical and directed interventions that do not bring about lasting, fruitful change.

Becoming Cynical

Cynicism is defined by the *Cambridge English Dictionary* as "the belief that people are only interested in themselves and are not sincere."[27] If there's a predominant view in society today, it's that government can't be trusted, they are in it for themselves, they're a bunch of thieves, they're all corrupt, they're all the same … the list goes on and on.

I have seen the reality of this cynicism up close during my time working on Parliament Hill. And to be honest, politicians have contributed to this attitude through their incessant negativity toward leaders from other political parties. You can only accuse your opponent of being corrupt for so long before some people will begin to believe you. The only problem is that your opponent is telling their supporters the same thing about you. So this narrative goes back and forth, and everyone gets infected by it. It's a lose-lose situation.

The most alarming aspect of the rise in cynicism toward government is that it seems to be most prevalent amongst Christians. If the government makes a decision that a Christian disagrees with, they almost immediately accuse that political leader of being evil, corrupt, or untrustworthy. Even if such an accusation might be right, the reflex to categorize everything we disagree with in these terms is wrong. There's something to be said for giving people the benefit of the doubt (even in politics), for taking time to listen and understand your opponent, and for even having empathy with well-meaning intentions. We can disagree with how to do something without slandering a person and maligning their motives.

Most people enter politics because they have a desire to make the country and their community a better place. Some believe that the power of government should be harnessed in order to achieve that objective, so they promote policies that lead to more government intervention and more government spending. Others believe that many of the problems in society are exacerbated by too much government, so they work to reduce the footprint of government in society, including the growth of government spending and reach of overregulation. But if you sit down and talk to them, you'll find that both of these camps have the same objective at heart: they want to find solutions to the problems they see every day.

When viewing government from a distance, this is not what you see. Instead, you often see strife, contention, arguing, debating, accusations, name-calling, and heckling. Question Period in our federal parliament buildings comes to mind. Every sitting day for forty-five minutes, the opposition parties pummel the government with questions. In actual fact, there is no realistic expectation of getting real answers. As a result, the whole exercise ends up becoming more of an accusation period than a question period.

Some of this is political theatre. Some of it is for the cameras. Some of it is to try and score political points. Some of it is an attempt to impress your party's narrative on today's media story so that tomorrow's headlines paint your party in a good light and your opponent's party in a negative one. Politicians have been saying for decades that our parliamentary system should be more respectful, more dialogue-oriented, and less combative. It seems like every election someone is promising to change the way politics works and to take some of the toxicity out of it. But it never lasts. Before long, the parties are right back at it.

Why? Because it works. There is a public appetite for confrontation and gaslighting your opponent. We can blame politicians for acting this way (and they do need to be responsible for their behaviour) and be critical of them when they do, but the cynical environment that pervades Canadian politics exists only because it is present at the grassroots level. If it were not so, the public wouldn't tolerate it. Instead, we feed off the very activity we claim to despise.

But what most Canadians don't see is that very few federal politicians actually share their cynicism. They're not only in Ottawa to make a constructive contribution to the country, but they recognize that their colleagues "across the aisle" are there for the same reason. There is rarely a time when, following a combative Question Period, Members of Parliament from one side don't go across to the other to chat with some of their colleagues. When the cameras are off, the cordiality returns.

At receptions on Parliament Hill, MPs and Senators of all stripes attend and are happy to chat with one another, share a drink, and even have a good laugh together. When tragedy strikes a parliamentarian or their family, you will find the entire parliament rallying around to encourage them, make statements in the House supporting them, or sending them messages of well-wishes. There is far more respect and humanity between opposing parliamentarians than most Canadians realize.

This is a strong thing to say, but it needs to be said. Our cynicism is the result of deception. Some of this deception is the result of the political games that are played, and some the result of our own spiritual immaturity. But none of it is good, and none of it makes us any the better for it. The sooner we shake off this ungodly spirit, the better. Jesus constantly portrayed to us that he was able to see the good in everyone. It doesn't mean we deny what is blatantly wrong, but we don't jump to conclusions and be categorical about things we have no way of knowing—like people's motives. Even as he hung on the cross dying, Jesus acknowledged that his oppressors had no idea what they were doing: *"Father, forgive them, for they know not what they do"* (Luke 23:34, ESV).

At a minimum, we should do the same. When we see things we don't agree with, we shouldn't assume that the motivations are evil. They sometimes are, but they usually aren't. And since we have no way of really knowing the difference, we should err on the side of love. We should bless our enemies, not curse them.

Why is this important? Because cynicism in the church toward politicians poisons the well from which the water of life is supposed to flow. It makes us spiritually dull and ineffective. It destroys faith, which works by love. It undermines everything that God wants to do in our lives and in our land. We will not shift the nation with this kind of attitude.

Becoming Conspiratorial

The third thing we must avoid in the public square is becoming conspiratorial. This is harder than it sounds because politics is an arena rife with rumours, accusations, and judgments, and these are the key ingredients of conspiracy theories.

Scripture is clear that as Christians, we aren't to entertain gossip, rumours, accusations, or slander, but for some reason, many still seem to fall into the trap of conspiracy theories that spring from this well. Perhaps we're looking for insight to explain what's going on. Perhaps it makes us feel more spiritual. Perhaps it's our inclination to always be on the lookout for the Antichrist, the mark of the Beast, and the impending approach of Armageddon. But whatever the reason, it's destructive.

A conspiracy theory is a belief or explanation that suggests that a covert, often sinister, plot by a group or individual is behind certain events, situations, or phenomena. These theories often rely on the idea that the official or mainstream explanations are not only incorrect but deliberately misleading.

Conspiratorial attitudes are those that take speculation and begin to treat it like fact, even if it involves slandering someone's character. The speculation leads to accusations levied against people we have often never met in person, never had a conversation with, and have no relationship with. This is a dangerous place to be.

As Christians, we are to be lovers of truth. We aren't to jump to conclusions, make accusations, or cast judgements when there is not ample, clear evidence available. We are to be as wise as serpents but as innocent as doves. It doesn't mean that we can't call out bad policy, misinformation, or injustice when we see it. It means we must be extremely careful not to attribute motives or intent to those who are involved. When we start to judge the hearts of people, we have usually gone too far.

Even in Christian circles we're not always going to agree with one another on the issues and the narrative behind them. Some interpret a situation one way, and some another. But our responsibility is to be committed to the process of growing in our understanding and seeing our lives come into conformity with the Word of God. We don't need to feel it is our responsibility to examine every allegation made against the government in an attempt to determine if it's accurate or not. These kinds of pursuits can distract us and consume valuable time and resources and lead to heated arguments.

Paul warned about this in 2 Timothy 2:23 when he said, *"But have nothing to do with foolish and ignorant speculations [useless disputes over unedifying, stupid controversies], since you know that they produce strife and give birth to quarrels"* (AMP). Obviously, Paul was talking about arguments to do with theology and doctrine, but the parallel with political conspiracies is striking. They are unedifying and produce strife and give birth to quarrels. They promote *"speculations rather than stewardship."*

These are strong words, and we should take them to heart. This is not a call to wage war against others who we believe are falling into a conspiracy theory. Rather, it's a call to walk humbly with one another and to strive to live at peace with one another, even when we disagree.

On a personal level, it's a call to be diligent to ensure that we don't find ourselves sinning against God and man by believing and sharing slanderous accusations, remembering that we will give an account for every word we speak (Matthew 12:36).

Believing in conspiracy theories will begin to make us ineffective in promoting constructive change to shift the nation for two reasons. First, they distract us from the real task at hand (impacting the nation and transforming society) by making it look like an impossible task. Who can promote change when all the strings are being pulled behind the scenes by some invisible cabal of evil men and women wielding an almost invincible level of power? Such a worldview leads to cynicism, contempt, and a feeling of powerlessness. It contributes to a decline in trust of persons in authority and in our societal institutions. All of these are deadly problems that will shift our society toward a very dark place rather than one more representative of the kingdom of light.

The second problem is that those who adhere to conspiracy theories have usually succumbed to the belief that the real threat to the nation comes from radical and directed change, as described in Chapter Three. As soon as we begin to believe that power exerted from the top down is more influential than power that comes from the bottom up, we will focus all of our efforts in that direction. It's like being lured down a dead-end street. In the end, we get nowhere.

Becoming Disillusioned

So, what do we do when we see obvious corrupt behaviour at the highest level? What do we do when we see leaders get away with things with no consequences? These things are real, so how do we not grow disillusioned when we see them?

The answer is two-fold. One, we must not lose our trust in our civic institutions: Parliament, our judicial system, our electoral system, and so on. These are a critical part of the infrastructure of a free and healthy society. If we become disillusioned and believe they are all rigged and corrupt, then we lose our ability to influence them and be a blessing to the nation. How can we run for public office if we believe all politicians are crooked? How do we engage in politics at all? We can't. We are left to stand on the sidelines to criticize, judge, and slander. That is not the way to shift a nation.

The second thing we must do is to not lose our confidence in God. We must always circle back to our deep conviction that the kingdom of God is constantly expanding on the earth, and we are agents of that kingdom. When change looks impossible, people of faith stand strong and hold fast to their confidence in the Father. We have been entrusted with the authority to bind hell on earth and to release heaven on earth. We hold the keys to bringing a bit of heaven to the world around us. We are the salt of the earth and, like Jesus said, if the salt loses its saltiness, it is good for nothing except to be *"thrown out and trampled under people's feet"* (Matthew 5:13b, ESV).

Our leaders are not perfect, and our institutions are not perfect. But finding flaws doesn't mean they are irreparably broken. It just means we have more work to do. So let's work to make them better, not tear them down further. Let's bring it to the Father in the secret place. Let's allow him to give us vision and faith and strategy and wisdom to make things better, not disparage them as unfixable. In midst of the darkness, let's be unwavering in our confidence that *"… the earth will be filled with the knowledge of the glory of the Lord as the waters cover the sea"* (Habakkuk 2:14, ESV).

To shift the nation, it's essential that we not fall into the trap of blaming the government for the ills in the country, becoming cynical, conspiratorial, or disillusioned. Being engaged in the public square carries with it a responsibility that we understand why we are there and what we should be doing, and a responsibility to know what kind of beliefs and behaviours will minimize our effectiveness and detract us from reaching our goal. There is much for us to learn about these matters, and there is no better way to learn than by embarking on the journey and letting our heavenly Father teach us along the way.

CHAPTER FOURTEEN

Christians in the Place of Prayer

WHEN THE JEWS went into exile in Babylon, God gave them specific instructions through the prophet Jeremiah: *"… seek the welfare of the city where I have sent you into exile, and pray to the Lord on its behalf, for in its welfare you will find your welfare"* (Jeremiah 29:7, ESV). The admonition was clear, and the scripture continues to speak to us today. We are to pray to the Lord on behalf of our nation, seeking its welfare.

But to do so effectively involves the embracing of two truths that at times can appear to contradict each other: government is both a mirror and a megaphone. As a mirror, government reflects back to us the state of the nation. It's not the source of the problems in our nation, but it mirrors back to us the existing state and brokenness of society. If we fail to recognize this, we will think that the government is the source of our societal problems, and we'll focus our attention on the symptoms without ever addressing the root. Yet as a megaphone, government has tremendous power to amplify voices and messages, which can then result in an increase of brokenness and destructive behaviour. So while it's not the root of the problem, it can be an amplifier of good or evil.

An excellent example of this is the issue of medical assistance in dying. In 2016, the federal government passed Bill C-14, *The Medical Assistance in Dying Act*. To the uninitiated it looked like the government was responsible for legalizing assisted suicide. Yet this was not the case. Rather, the change was driven by a 2015 Supreme Court decision in *Carter v. Canada (Attorney General)*. This court decision had overturned a Supreme Court decision made more than twenty years earlier that rejected arguments to make assisted suicide legal. Then, two decades later, the court reversed that decision.

The Court's decision was less than satisfactory in its explanation, but one key component of their justification for reversing course was this: society's view on this issue had shifted. What was once largely rejected by society was now more broadly accepted. The Court decided to strike down the existing legislation governing assisted suicide and, as a result, Parliament had to re-write the law to come in line with the court decision. In other words, the legislation was mirroring the existing state and brokenness of the nation.

It wasn't long, however, until the government began advocating to expand the restrictive boundaries that the Court had placed on medical assistance in dying. The government rejected key amendments to try and protect the vulnerable and indicated that they would even be willing to consider medical assistance in dying for mental health issues. The parameters began moving out far beyond what the Supreme Court's decision seemed to anticipate. This is what it looks like when the government becomes a megaphone. It no longer merely mirrors the state of the nation but amplifies a certain position, which threatens to move public policy far beyond mainstream public opinion.

Because government can be a mirror and a megaphone, a balanced, strategic approach to prayer must recognize both of these truths. If we fail in this, then our prayers will fall to one extreme or the other. Either government will be the sole focus of our prayers, or we will see no purpose to pray for the government. Both are limited in their effectiveness.

STRATEGIES FOR EFFECTIVE PRAYER

An untold number of books have been written on the subject of prayer. But in spite of this, prayer seems to remain a mystery for many Christians. We know we're supposed to pray, but we're not sure why. After all, what's the purpose of prayer if God knows everything already? And didn't Jesus say in Matthew 6:8, "*… your Father knows what you need before you ask him*" (ESV)? Since God is all powerful, why doesn't he just do what needs to be done? Why do we need to pray?

Part Two laid a critical foundation for understanding the answers to these questions. Knowing that God holds all authority but has chosen to partner with us in order to see things happen suddenly causes us to see prayer in a different perspective. It starts to make sense. We realize that intercessory prayer is not trying to convince God of things, but rather we are partnering with him to see his kingdom come and his will be done.

When it comes to prayer strategies to shift a nation, we need to focus on the right things. Focusing on specific things doesn't exclude others, but it gives us our priority in prayer and our priority for evaluating our progress. And they all reach back to the understanding laid out in Chapter Four, that effective, long-lasting change is incremental and organic.

Here's how this applies to prayer:

1. Focus on Organic, Not Directed Change

When we pray, we should focus on organic change, not directed change. Jesus' examples of the kingdom of God were largely organic in nature: a tree growing, a farmer sowing, an investment multiplying. These are all things that grow over time.

Applying this to praying about government and the nation shows us that we should primarily focus our prayers on people, not programs or policies. This is largely the opposite of what the church in Canada has been doing.

Let's once again take the example of the law concerning assisted suicide. When the Liberal government introduced this legislation, prayer groups across the nation immediately focused their prayers on seeing the bill defeated. When it became clear that this wasn't going to happen, they focused on amendments to make the bill less harmful. This didn't happen either. In spite of how well-meaning such an approach may have been, it's a good example of ineffective prayer. Allow me to explain.

When government legislation gets introduced in Parliament, it's usually the end of the process, not the beginning. Governments introduce legislation they believe reflects the will of the electorate, and especially those who put them into office. They will never introduce legislation that they believe will be defeated—at least not purposefully. So when bad legislation shows up in Parliament, it's like the tip of the iceberg. There is a huge mass below the water level that you can't see. You can fire away at the visible tip of the iceberg until that tip is gone, but it still lurks below the surface and is large enough to still sink the *Titanic* if it runs into it. Praying against legislation is about the most ineffective practice of prayer that can be undertaken. And it almost always results in failure.

Legislation is a reflection of the beliefs and values of the nation. If it doesn't accurately reflect these beliefs and values, it won't survive and be passed into law. Trying to defeat legislation by praying that God causes it to be defeated in Parliament shows that we are invested in pursuing radical and directed change, not incremental and organic change. It's the opposite of what we should be doing if we want to be effective.

Christians tend to approach elections the same way. We think that if we pray hard enough, God will cause the right leader to win the election. It's another attempt to force radical and directed change, and it's a recipe for frustration and discouragement. It amazes me how many times the church in Canada has managed to muster up the energy to pray fervently against a certain political party, only to have that party win. Christians often face disappointment after the election but then fail to glean any insights from the experience. Instead, at the next election, new reasons are floated about why it didn't work last time but will work this time, and the process starts all over.

Elections are won and lost based on how people vote. And God does not override the free will of people and force their hand in the ballot box to mark a candidate they never intended to support. This doesn't mean we shouldn't be praying for elections. But when we do, our prayers should be focused on change that is organic, not directed. If we want to affect election outcomes, we must impact the beliefs and values of the people voting. This is the only way to see a shift, and this takes time.

Whether we like it or not, nations change when people change—not the other way around. Likewise, laws change when people change. And that is exactly what has been happening in Canada. The laws we have today are a direct reflection of how the beliefs and values of our nation have changed over the past few decades. And that is the primary reason why our prayers should be focused on people, not policies.

The Apostle Paul gives us a good illustration of this in how he handled things at Ephesus. This city was overrun with witchcraft, magic, sorcery, and the like, yet you don't see Paul walk into the city and start trying to deal with those ungodly practices. Instead, he started teaching in the synagogue. And when he was thrown out of there after three months, he went to another location in the city and carried on discipling the believers for two years.

> Also many of those who were now believers came, confessing and divulging their practices. And a number of those who had practiced magic arts brought their books together and burned them in the sight of all. And they counted the value of them and found it came to fifty thousand pieces of silver. (Acts 19:18–19, ESV)

Fifty thousand pieces of silver in Paul's day is estimated to be the equivalent of about $5.5 million dollars today. Paul chose to address the matters of the heart, and the result was a huge purging of witchcraft and sorcery in the city.

If you dropped twenty-first-century Canadian Christians into this same environment, we probably would have retreated to the basement of a church somewhere to pray that God would make witchcraft illegal. We would have had great prayer meetings and intense worship, and maybe fired off some form-letter emails to politicians, but it would have changed nothing. To be effective in praying for our nation, we need to focus primarily on people, not policies. Change must be organic, not directed, and to be effective, our prayers should reflect that same pattern.

2. Focus on Incremental, Not Radical Change

When we pray for our nation, we should focus on incremental, not radical, change. Whether we like it or not, change in the kingdom of God usually manifests in increments. Not always, but most often, God works from "glory to glory" and "line upon line."

Consider that Abraham was to become the father of a great nation, yet God gave him only one son. And then that son had only two sons. Jesus came to establish the kingdom of heaven on the earth and started with twelve disciples. He said he'd be right back, and he's been gone for almost two thousand years. God is very incremental in his work, and our prayers should mirror this priority. It's not that there aren't seismic shifts, but these are usually the result of incremental movements that have been compounding over time.

When applying this to praying for our nation, it means we should be focusing our prayers on the journey, not the destination. In other words, what's the next step? What is the heart of the matter? For example, if the church was flowing in the power of the Spirit and divine healing was a common occurrence like it was with Jesus, would people be asking for medical assistance in dying? Perhaps the popularity of assisted suicide is the direct result of the church's failure to fully apprehend the promise of healing. Perhaps instead of looking at the government we should be looking at ourselves and contending in prayer for the church to begin to move in a powerful healing anointing. Perhaps the rot in society is the result of the church having lost its saltiness.

These are the kinds of questions we need to ask ourselves. Instead of praying against the end result, we should be focusing on the next step in the right direction so that our prayers are more targeted, more strategic, more incremental, and more effective. It's not that we should never pray about the big picture, but we shouldn't kid ourselves into thinking that the solution is found in change that is radical and directed. Lasting change is organic and incremental, and that is where our prayers should be primarily focused.

3. Every Change Involves a Transition and a Trigger

A transition and a trigger means that there is something that must change, but there is also something that causes that change. Instead of focusing our prayers on what needs to change, we should allow the Spirit of God to direct us to pray for what will cause that change. Focus on the trigger and not the transition.

Consider the parable Jesus told in Matthew 25:14–30. This is the story of the man who was going on a journey and entrusted his servants with his gold. When the master returned, the servants were judged based on the increase in the wealth under their stewardship. Two of them did very well and doubled the finances under their care. The third servant failed to see any kind of increase and was reprimanded for it. In this case, the desired outcome was to see an increase in the resources that had been entrusted to them. But the trigger was investing and doing business wisely. If they invested wisely, they would see an increase. If they did not (like the third servant) then there was no increase.

In the context of prayer, the proper strategy wouldn't be to pray for increase (the desired outcome or the "transition"). It would be to pray for wise investment strategies and opportunities—the "trigger" that will bring about the desired outcome.

In Luke 10:2, Jesus tells his followers, *"The harvest is plentiful, but the workers are few. Ask the Lord of the harvest, therefore, to send out workers into his harvest field"* (NIV). The desired outcome (the transition) is a successful harvest. But Jesus instructs his disciples to pray for more workers, because this was the key, or the trigger, to seeing the desired outcome become a reality.

This may sound simple, but it's significant. As Christians praying for the nation, we tend to get preoccupied with praying for the desired outcome when we should be focused more on what will bring that outcome about. Granted, this is not always easy to discern. Sometimes the trigger is not what we think. But this is where we need to look to the Holy Spirit to give us insight, wisdom, and strategy. Because this is how our partnership with God works in prayer.

4. Every Change Has a Root and a Result

Every change has a root and a result. The root is what caused the situation, and the result is what you see that needs to change. Jesus constantly focused on the root, knowing that if it was dealt with, that would bring about the desired result: *"A good person produces good things from the treasury of a good heart, and an evil person produces evil things from the treasury of an evil heart"* (Luke 6:45). Jesus knew that if you change the heart, you'll change what comes out of it. He wasn't focused on behaviour modification; he was focused on getting to the root of the matter.

We see this again in John 14:15, when Jesus tells his disciples, *"If you love me, you will keep my commandments"* (ESV). He didn't say, "If you keep my commandments, you will love me." It was the opposite: focus on loving me, because that is going to result in you keeping my commandments. Jesus knew that when the root is healthy, the result will be desirable.

When applying this to prayer, we need to ask the Holy Spirit to show us the roots of situations and then direct our prayers there. It's easy to get caught up praying about the way things are and asking God to change them when we should be focused on the root of the matter. If we change the root, we will change the fruit.

It's imperative that we pray for our nation and for the government of our nation. In fact, we are commanded to do so in 1 Timothy 2:1–2:

> First of all, then, I urge that supplications, prayers, intercessions, and thanksgivings be made for all people, for kings and all who are in high positions, that we may lead a peaceful and quiet life, godly and dignified in every way. (ESV)

We must acknowledge that our track record of effectiveness in prayer for our nation has been limited. There are many reasons for this, but among them is the fact that the church is usually attempting to use prayer to impose things on the nation, rather than taking an organic and incremental approach to our prayer strategy. If we implement these four simple points above, it will cause us to be more effective and fruitful in prayer for our nation.

CONCLUSION

IF CHRISTIANS WANT to be effective in shifting the nation, we need to change our approach. Up to this point, our efforts have been largely aimed at either preserving or restoring our previously held favoured position in the state. This is simply not going to work, and the sooner we realize it, the more effective we'll be. The key to transforming society is not top-down, but bottom-up. It's organic and incremental change that creates constructive, sustainable shifts in a nation. This is not only the historical record but the biblical model taught by Jesus and demonstrated throughout the Bible. It is the pattern we are to follow, and it's our mandate from heaven.

That doesn't mean it will be easy. In fact, some seasons can be quite difficult. I remember one day while I was working with the Centre for Prairie Agriculture and finances were very tight, I went for a job interview. We had a young family and were behind on all of our financial obligations, so I felt that I had no choice but to leave the organization I had helped to found and go look for other employment.

As the job interview progressed, I heard God speak to me very clearly. He said, "What are you doing here?" He didn't need to explain, and he didn't say another word. I knew exactly what he meant. He hadn't told me to go and look for another job, so why was I there? Despite the financial challenges we were facing, giving up and walking away was not an option. I politely ended the job interview and went back to the office.

Sometimes on the journey of life, victory is simply showing up. This was one of those days. There was no big breakthrough, no miracle, no sudden turn-around, and no change. I went back to work and put my shoulder to the wheel. To be honest, there were many days like that. We were acting out of obedience to God and a passion to see him shift things for prairie farmers. At the time, things were so difficult in the prairie grain industry that farmers were committing suicide. Government policy was contributing to this despair, and it needed to change. God would not let us abandon our post, and we faithfully set our hearts to carry it out, regardless of the cost.

Over the years, our journey took many turns. It would take us from Regina, to Edmonton, to Victoria, back to Regina, back to Edmonton, and finally off to the nation's capital. In Ottawa I would work as a political staffer, first in the House of Commons and then in the Senate, progressing through the ranks from Legislative Assistant for a Member of Parliament to Director of Policy for the Leader of the Opposition in the Senate. We weren't always certain of the strategy, but we never veered from what God was speaking to us. As those who have tasted of his goodness, we must be present in the city gates and in the marketplace.

A few years ago, God directed my wife, Gail, to work at Walmart. She had previously worked in administrative roles both with a non-profit organization and on Parliament Hill, first for a Member of Parliament and then later for the Office of the Leader of the Opposition. But now God was directing her to Walmart.

The strategy was very simple: go and work where the people of your community gather and bring the presence and the goodness of God into that environment. On the first day of the job, Gail came home and said to me, "I learned today that for most people, a little hope is a lot of hope, a little joy is a lot of joy, and a little encouragement is a lot of encouragement." She had immediately seen the need and how she could make a difference.

Over the next few years, Gail would touch the lives of thousands of people who went through her checkout. Sometimes in small ways, and sometimes in large ways, such as having them see direct answers to prayer after she prayed for them. But no matter how seemingly small an encounter may seem to be, you can't underestimate the significance of the impact. How do you know if the person you just encouraged was not considering self-harm before you lifted their spirits? How do you know if that parent went home and was a better mom or dad because they felt an unexplainable peace come over them after chatting briefly with the cashier at Walmart? How do you know if you just thwarted the plans of the enemy for a person's life by speaking hope and value to them?

During the COVID lockdowns, Walmart was the one place people could always go. And Gail worked through it all. Seniors would come through who were lonely and isolated. Gail would encourage them to come see her as often as they needed to because she could see that they would leave a little bit lighter and a little more hopeful. Children would come through with their parents, and everyone was stressed. Gail would engage the kids, cheer them up, and everyone left happier.

It's hard work. Packing groceries, engaging people, being "up" and encouraging all the time. Gail comes home exhausted. But she loves it because it's caring for the community, and we have both seen and felt a change in the atmosphere of the store.

Over the past few years, I've made a point of occasionally going into Walmart and just watching Gail work without her knowing I'm there. I love watching her encourage people, watching her serve people, watching her let people know they're valued and that they matter. If someone is struggling, she'll tell them that she'll pray for them and ask them to come back and let her know if things improve. And they do. She always has a smile and is always looking for ways to lift their spirits and words to encourage them. And she is constantly praying for them, even when they don't know it. She's on a mission, and I can sense the Father's pleasure in it all.

In spite of opportunities to advance, Gail has felt to remain in the role of a cashier. She could be somewhere else, making more money and climbing the corporate ladder. But for now, this is where she has been assigned by the Father, because this is where he wants her to touch the lives of hundreds of people every day.

I share this story to make a very simple point. It doesn't matter if you work in the Parliament of Canada or at Walmart—you have a significant role to play in shifting the nation. Shifting the nation is not a job for someone else. It is a job for all of us.

But we cannot simply continue to do what we've always done and expect different results. To shift the nation, we must shift and begin to embrace God's strategy for change. My prayer is that this book has left you with a greater understanding of that strategy, and a greater hunger to pursue it. Because together, God can use us to shift the nation.

ABOUT THE AUTHOR

CRAIG DOCKSTEADER IS a pastor whom God called to go on an adventure in the public square. From serving as the Senior Operations Officer of the Canadian Taxpayers Federation to working as Director of Policy in the Office of the Leader of the Opposition in the Senate of Canada, Craig's journey has yielded invaluable insight into understanding the church's role in addressing the challenges facing our nation. Craig has been happily married to Gail for over 38 years, has three daughters, one son-in-law, six grandchildren, and currently lives in Ottawa, Canada.

For more resources, visit www.ToShiftANation.ca.

ENDNOTES

[1] Richard Moon, "Government Support for Religious Practice," *Law and Religious Pluralism in Canada* (Vancouver, BC: UBC Press, 2008). Available at SSRN: https://ssrn.com/abstract=1866489.

[2] Mouvement laïque québécois v. Saguenay (City), 2015 SCC 16, [2015] 2 S.C.R. 3, Supreme Court of Canada, https://scc-csc.lexum.com/scc-csc/scc-csc/en/item/15288/index.do.

[3] "2. Historical Trends | Ontario Human Rights Commission," Ontario Human Rights Commission, Ohrc.on.ca. 2012. https://www.ohrc.on.ca/en/iii-background-and-context/2-historical-trends, accessed November 24, 2023.

[4] It needs to be acknowledged that the good intentions and actions of the early Christian church in Canada in no way excuse the wrongs and abuses that occurred, such as clearly seen in the harmful legacy of residential schools. These wrongs were not only reprehensible and regrettable, but they graphically illustrate the harm that comes from efforts to impose change on others rather than understanding how constructive change takes place in a nation.

[5] Troy Lanigan, *Fighting for Taxpayers* (Regina, SK: The Canadian Taxpayers Federation, 2015).

[6] "Now Is the Time for a 'Great reset,'" World Economic Forum, June 3, 2020, accessed November 24, 2023, https://www.weforum.org/agenda/2020/06/now-is-the-time-for-a-great-reset/

[7] Greta Thunberg, "Transcript: Greta Thunberg's Speech at the U.N. Climate Action Summit," NPR, September 23, 2019, accessed November 24, 2023, https://www.npr.org/2019/09/23/763452863/transcript-greta-thunbergs-speech-at-the-u-n-climate-action-summit.

[8] I am keenly aware that some of these scriptures and statements may seem to contradict some of the popular end times theology of our day. This is not my intent. Nor do I believe it is necessary for the purposes of what we are considering in these pages. There is much disagreement over which eschatology is the correct one, and

I have no interest in engaging in those debates in these pages. I believe that we can and should embrace the clear teachings of scripture, without needing to first have absolute clarity on those things that are unclear. And it is clear that while Jesus has been given all authority, he is not yet exercising that authority in full but is in the process of bringing all things under his feet. That much of an understanding is critical, and it is enough for us to move forward in our journey to understanding how to effectively promote constructive change within our nation.

[9] Schuyler Signor, "The Third Person Imperative in the Greek New Testament," 1999, Academia, 33, accessed November 30, 2023, https://www.academia.edu/30199594/THE_THIRD_PERSON_IMPERATIVE_IN_THE_GREEK_NEW_TESTAMENT

[10] Rodney Stark, *The Rise of Christianity: How the Obscure, Marginal Jesus Movement Became the Dominant Religious Force in the Western World in a Few Centuries* (San Francisco, CA: HarperCollins, 1997).

[11] Ibid., 20.

[12] Ibid.

[13] Ibid., 56.

[14] Ibid., 86.

[15] Ibid., 86.

[16] Ibid., 73.

[17] Ibid., 82.

[18] Ibid.

[19] Ibid., 82.

[20] Ibid., 83.

[21] Ibid., 91.

[22] Ibid., 95.

[23] Mouvement laïque québécois v. Saguenay (City), 2015 SCC 16, [2015] 2 S.C.R. 3 https://scc-csc.lexum.com/scc-csc/scc-csc/en/item/15288/index.do

[24] Ibid., 74.

[25] Ibid., Para 71.

[26] Ibid., Para 137.

[27] *Cambridge English Dictionary*, s.v. "cynicism," accessed November 10, 2023, https://dictionary.cambridge.org/us/dictionary/english/cynicism.

BIBLIOGRAPHY

Lanigan, Troy. *Fighting for Taxpayers*. Regina, SK: The Canadian Taxpayers Federation, 2015.

Moon, Richard. "Government Support for Religious Practice." *Law and Religious Pluralism in Canada*. Vancouver, BC: UBC Press, 2008. Available at SSRN: https://ssrn.com/abstract=1866489.

NPR. Thunberg, Greta. "Transcript: Greta Thunberg's Speech at the U.N. Climate Action Summit." https://www.npr.org/2019/09/23/763452863/transcript-greta-thunbergs-speech-at-the-u-n-climate-action-summit.

Ontario Human Rights Commission. "2. Historical Trends | Ontario Human Rights Commission." Ohrc.on.ca. 2012. https://www.ohrc.on.ca/en/iii-background-and-context/2-historical-trends

Signor, Schuyler. "The Third Person Imperative in the Greek New Testament." 1999. Academia. https://www.academia.edu/30199594/THE_THIRD_PERSON_IMPERATIVE_IN_THE_GREEK_NEW_TESTAMENT.

Stark, Rodney. *The Rise of Christianity: How the Obscure, Marginal Jesus Movement Became the Dominant Religious Force in the Western World in a Few Centuries*. San Francisco, CA: HarperCollins, 1997.

Supreme Court of Canada. Mouvement laïque québécois v. Saguenay (City), 2015 SCC 16, [2015] 2 S.C.R. 3. https://scc-csc.lexum.com/scc-csc/scc-csc/en/item/15288/index.do.

World Economic Forum. "Now Is the Time for a 'Great reset.'" June 3, 2020. https://www.weforum.org/agenda/2020/06/now-is-the-time-for-a-great-reset/.

www.ingramcontent.com/pod-product-compliance
Lightning Source LLC
LaVergne TN
LVHW051408080426
835508LV00022B/2990